When we came to Week

Margaret R Bolt

Best wishes
Margaret Bolt.

First published 2001 by
Edward Gaskell Publishers
Cranford House
6 Grenville Street
Bideford
Devon EX39 2EA

Designed by Jane Pearce

isbn 1-898546-49-5

When We Came To Week

Margaret R Bolt

Printed and bound by
Lazarus Press
Unit 7 Caddsdown Business Park
Bideford
Devon EX39 3DX

I dedicate this book to the memory of our grandson,
Paul John Manning, 1977 – 1983
who loved this farm;

to my parents and grandparents
who formed my past;

to my dear husband Eric
who is my here and now;

and to my daughters Kathleen and Hazel
and their husbands and children,
for the future is theirs
to mould as they wish.

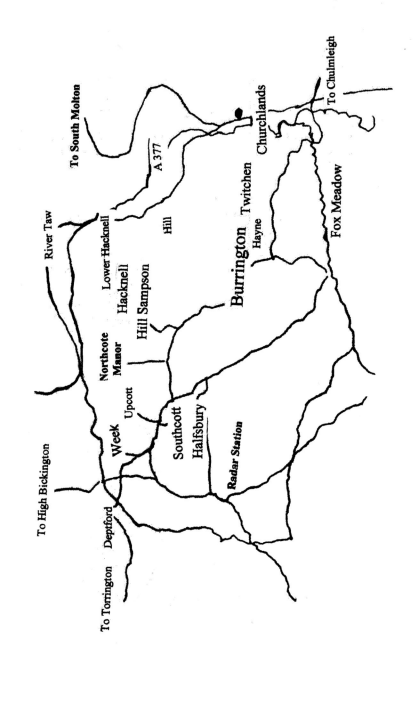

CONTENTS

This was repeated to me by Mrs. Parkhouse of Fox Meadow,
when she heard we were to be farming Week.

"Out to Week amongst the trees,
Barley bread and vinnied cheese,
Risty bacon as tough as a thong,
That's how Week boys live along"

PREFACE

This book came about after Kathleen and Hazel, having heard me say for the umpteenth time "When we came to Week ...." encouraged the recording of that now distant age for them and future generations.

So began, in March 1996, a series of articles in the Burrington and High Bickington parish magazines to celebrate the fiftieth anniversary of coming to Week.

After only a few had been printed, readers began to ask when a book was being published! Little did I imagine that enough memories could be recalled to make this worthwhile and that six years later it would have such a dramatic ending.

I thank all who have encouraged me to carry on writing by their kind comments and offers of help. For a few corrections from those with better memories than I have – and more years to remember! But most of all I must thank my friend, Jane Pearce, for her tireless patience in typing and retyping each scribbled hand written article while I switched sentences around – then back again! I must thank her for taking, and scanning photographs; and for presenting the whole manuscript on disc to Lazarus Press ready for printing and binding. Without her help I would have given up long ago.

Thanks to Robin Ravilious for use of her drawing of the French Ales and to Beaford Archives for the use of the two photographs of cider making at Hacknell, taken by James Ravilious when my father and uncles were nearing the end of their cider-making years.

Week

INTRODUCTION

Burrington is a parish in North Devon, rising to over 600 feet at Burrington Moor in the south and bounded by the Mully Brook flowing eastwards to join the River Taw at Hansford. This river is then the northern boundary as far as Kingford, a hamlet on the A.377 Exeter to Barnstaple road.

A stream criss-crossing under Kingford Hill is the western edge, rising to Week Parks Cross from where roads, streams and hedges bring one back to Burrington Moor, a distance of fifteen to sixteen miles. Dartmoor and Exmoor are easily visible from this area on clear days and the wind blows across it from every direction; but within the parish are sheltered valleys, farm houses down deep lanes, acres of rich fertile land as well as areas of rushy culm grassland. A parish it has been my privilege to have lived in all my life.

Hacknell and Week were part of the Northcote estate until Col. Gracey's death in 1962. As "sitting" tenant my father bought Week, his brothers Abie and John bought Hacknell, continuing farming there until Abie's sudden death in 1978.

The farm was sold that year, bringing an end to Eastmans at Hacknell, after forty-six years. Now, Tim and Jo Budden with their three children farm there, in much the same way as my grandfather did in the 1930s, but with the aid of modern machinery and technology.

Family Tree

Alice Maud Way	m	Albert Eastman

George	Albert (Abie)	John	Bernard

Emily Webber	m	George Hewitt

Rose	Doris	Cissie	Ted	Phyllis	Muriel	Edith	Evelyn

Margaret	m	Eric Bolt

David Manning	m	Kathleen		Hazel	m	David Pearce

Paul b. 02.07.77	Fiona b. 04.10.86	James b. 10.05.88	Megan b. 01.01.00	due Jan 02

WHY WE CAME TO WEEK

Lady Day 1946 my father, George Eastman, became a tenant of Col.Thomas Gracey of Northcote Manor, who had bought Week Farm, Burrington in 1945 from William Pincombe of Bishopstawton. A near relative (I think nephew), Alfred Pincombe, became the tenant at Week in 1906. Farming through two world wars and the thirties depression he retired after 40 years, which made him very ancient viewed through the eyes of a child.

Col. Gracey already owned Higher Week, with Bob Underhill following his father as tenant. The fields of the two farms were very intermixed so by owning both, he could swap acreages around to make convenient blocks of land.

Col. Gracey

*Bob Underhill
and his father*

11

Before coming to Week we lived at Hacknell with my grandparents, Bert and Maud Eastman, and three Uncles, Abie, John and Bernie. In the early 40s my father worked for John Snell, licencee and farmer at Portsmouth Arms before working for Jim Pincombe at Abbotsmarsh until early Spring, 1946. Bernie, aged 17 and employed at Murch Bros., Umberleigh, decided to come to Week with us.

Aerial view of Higher Hacknell, 1960s. The stable being the only remaining thatched building

In March 1946, less than a year after the end of World War II, petrol, sweets and basic foodstuffs were still rationed – but not bread; bread units came later. Clothing was controlled by coupons; it was the era of make do and mend. I cannot remember any jumble sales. Clothes were worn until they were outgrown, then passed on, or if too frail to mend again were hung by the back door because "they might come in useful" for the dog to lie on, or dressing a scarecrow! Bedding and new furniture were only available with dockets, issued mainly to newly-weds and when babies arrived, so we did not qualify on either count.

Mum had great difficulty furnishing a five-bedroomed house. Although recovering from a bad attack of pleurisy, she went to local house clearance sales to buy second-hand furnishings. Scarcity obviously made prices high. She bought as many things as Mrs. Pincombe was willing to leave behind at Week – and that she could afford. We still have some blue lino – now in the dairy – a chest of drawers and a wall clock from the Pincombes, a glass cupboard from "Keeper" Turner's sale at Golden Haven and a wooden chest from Tom Mills' sale at South Down. Mrs. Gracey gave Mum two pairs of sheets, laundry dated 1939 and Mrs. Short – Hillcrest – gave her a pair of gold brocade curtains.

A few other pieces of furniture came from a cottage at Winswood; these had been loaned by Mrs. Gracey to the Sorrells, an evacuee family, helping to furnish their home whilst in Burrington, but they having recently returned to London the furniture was there for collecting – a gift from Mrs. Gracey. Badly damaged but still welcome to relieve the unfurnished look at Week. Tom Friend repaired the broken in half, small, square dining table for the sitting room and later made three long forms (benches) to replace the ones left by Mrs. Pincombe which were in danger of collapse whenever we moved them on the rough concrete floor in the kitchen. Made to measure to provide seating around the old kitchen table left by Mrs. Pincombe, two are still in constant use, although that table was replaced ten years later by an extending polished mahogany one, easily moved on castors. The old table was unusual in that the top and base were not joined together. Each solid square leg was joined top and bottom at right angles to its neighbour on either side by a mortice and tenon-jointed, very stout rail, making a sturdy but extremely heavy construction. The wider and longer heavy top, smooth on both sides, could be slid on the base to make eating comfortable for small children or larger adults alike, on the other hand, a nasty surprise was in store for anyone resting their bottom and weight against the edge, only to discover their support rapidly disappear!

Also left behind by the Sorrells were a few hens of various ages. One was obviously young for we kept her for several years. Free to roam she became very tame, responding eagerly when called by her name, Doris, after the Sorrells daughter. This hen struck up an unusual friendship with a large tabby tom cat left by the Pincombes; it was amusing to see this golden feathered hen and the grey cat parading around the yard leaning into each other.

At Hacknell in the sitting room the large cupboard under the stairs where Granny Eastman kept spare china was considerably reduced when a little girl was given the task of packing any surplus in a barrel layered with straw. We still have a few 1937 King George VI coronation mugs, bought after the event at Woolworth's for 1d each and used on threshing days. Granny also gave me two cups and saucers, one "A present from Honiton", the other from Chard, now cherished pieces in our collection of local souvenir ware begun in 1980. Any offers of household goods, however ancient, were eagerly accepted from friends and distant relatives. Being part of an extended family was very useful!

HACKNELL

Although excited at the thought of moving to Week, there was sorrow to be leaving Hacknell, the only home I had ever known, with the familiar and well loved things there.

View from Hill Sampson – Hacknell lower right

The house is set in a hollow on the north facing side of the Taw Valley. Descending the lane views of fields on the Chittlehamholt side spread out before you looking –without too much imagination – like toy farms in the distance. From the house, the plum garden and orchard were the extent of the view, with the exception of one bedroom facing east where there was a panoramic view in the direction of Kingsnympton. From the enclosed farmyard at the back of the house a narrower version of this scene was visible over a gate, between two buildings.

Hacknell today

The house at Hacknell was of simple construction – a long oblong, one room wide, entered either through the front door from the garden or the back door, approached up a step from the farm yard and enclosed back yard. The wide front door protected from the weather by a small gabled porch, opened into the living room/kitchen, with the stairs rising straight ahead, only visible if the high stair door was open.

To the left a door opened into the sitting room, large and square, as were all four downstair rooms. The only room with a wood floor, partly covered by a carpet square, it had wainscotting halfway up the wall, the top being wallpapered. A small grate off-centre in the end wall warmed that corner of the room; the rest was kept cool by draughts blowing around the window and doors into the room and from the cupboard under the stairs. Used every evening during winter by some of the family, Granfer usually read the paper or Farmer and Stockbreeder, Mum and Gran knitted or darned socks before playing cards until bedtime. It was there I learnt to play whist.

The adjoining room was the most used room of the house; here the very long kitchen table almost filled the front wall from the door, with a full length fixed bench under the window and a moveable form the other side. Sixteen men could be seated here comfortably when reed combing. Granfer sat in a wood carver type armchair at the end of the table.

16

The drawer underneath and the bracket on the calendar behind him were for years all the office storage space he needed, until he eventually had a desk in the sitting room. Beside his chair on the piece of fitted bench beyond the table, Granny's Singer sewing machine was kept, convenient to be used on the table when needed. The far end of the table was used for ironing, oilcloth folded back, the bare wood was protected by an old blanket to prevent scorching. We sat around the table on winter evenings to play Snap, Ludo, Draughts, Drive the Old Woman to Bed, Snakes and Ladders and Shove ha'penny, by the light of a Tilley lamp stood on the table.

Beyond Granfer's chair, above the door opening into the back kitchen, a gun rack hung where several twelve bore shotguns were kept and on the door a dart board was fixed, darts being another winter pastime. Spars for thatching were split from hazel gads beside the open fire, the waste easily brushed up on the bare floor adding more fuel to the fire.

Next came a kitchen cabinet where foodstuffs in use and everyday china were stored. Half the back wall was taken up by the open fireplace, complete with the frequently used oven in the wall. Above the fireplace the mantelpiece or shelf with a pelmet hanging from the edge provided dry storage for cartridges etc. An old sofa filled the space from the fire to a glass cupboard, the top displayed best china, the bottom stored all kinds of odds and ends accumulated in most households.

Next a small narrow table supported the wireless, attached to its wet and dry batteries and long aerial leading from the house across the lane to end high up in a large oak tree on the bank opposite.

There I had been led to believe years before that pianos and orchestras were being played, which had always disappeared by the time I got there, much to the amusement of "the boys".

I remember the outbreak of war being announced on that wireless on September 3rd, 1939.

*Me and poultry rearing
equipment with the
large tree on the bank
where I believed the
B.B.C. programmes
came from.*

The grandfather clock also stood against this stair wall and for some reason in its base was always kept a bottle of elderberry wine, used as medicine for coughs and colds. A runner of threadbare carpet and a few wood chairs completed the furnishings in that room. There were no chairs in the back kitchen. Behind the door on which a long roller towel hung the chopping block and hatchet were kept along with faggots and "hard" wood brought in from the wood rick ('ood rick) at the entrance to the mowstead.

A cupboard in the corner, where boots and shoes were kept and cleaned, stood next to the scrubbed-top table below the window, on which vegetables were prepared, pastry made, cakes mixed and dishes washed – in a pan of hot water, left to drain on a metal tray, a block of Bath brick on the windowsill, ready to hand for cleaning the steel cutlery. The Monday wash took place in trays resting on the bench kept under this table.

The furnace wash boiler was installed in the corner, with space for someone to stand between it and the blue slate slab on brick pillars, to turn the handle of the old cream separator fixed to this slab. Consisting of numerous cups which had to be assembled in an exact pattern to work at all, separating was a tedious, arm aching job.

In the small corner between the dairy and back doors was a three section wood orange box, stood on end, used as storage for best boots and leggings. Along the back wall was a tap from the reservoir and a large pump for drinking water, the underfloor pipe supplying it crossing the garden and orchard from the meadow beyond.

A dark brown shallow sink made sure that anyone standing before it when the pump, for drinking water, was in use had a cold wet front. Later an overchurn milk cooler stood by this sink, a very hard working concern, for a churn stood on the ground below the corrugated metal cooler through which a continuous supply of cold water was tubed from the tap. Above all this was a bowl into which buckets of milk brought from the shippon were poured, to flow down over the cooler into the churn below, the flow adjusted by a tap on the bowl, and churns removed when full.

An oil burning cooker had replaced a former black Bodley along the remaining section of wall back to the middle door. Neither were very efficient or reliable, the Bodley relegated outdoors stayed under the dairy window for a long time – ideal for children to "cook" 'mucksy pies' in discarded tins for make believe tea parties.

The fourth and even colder room was the dairy which surprisingly had a large open fireplace, never lit, only used to provide yet more storage. Two walls had cold slate slabs, with shelves over, where pans of milk and joints of cooked meat rested. The trenells and salters of pork and bacon were in this room along with a small barrel of apples layered in straw – the main apple store was in the barn under an old barn thresher – the flour hutch with flour bought by the sack, a cupboard of wood and zinc used to store pots and pans and a large central table, under which baskets and anything needing a home were kept. A flush toilet very convenient for everyone was part of the back porch.

Upstairs had been a repeat of the four rooms downstairs until the west end room was divided to make a smaller bedroom – always the spare or guest room – and a good sized bathroom, with hot water tank in the large airing cupboard. The bath was a massive affair, free-standing, rolled end and supported on claw feet, the kind interior designers today dream about.

The opposite end of the house was the largest bedroom. This was the "boys" room with two double beds and one singe. Next door another divided room, part of which had been a windowless boxroom, then my sleeping quarters adjoining Mum and Dad's bedroom. A window was provided in this room when we had the three Harris children evacuees. Jean and Joyce shared that room with me, a double and single bed almost filling the space.

Our evacuees from Tottenham,
Joyce, Jean and Willie Harris, outside
Michael's Photographers, Market Street, Barnstaple

The fourth room was Granny and Granfer's, which like all the rest had no ceiling and attic above it. The roof structure of huge cross-beams supporting a central upright pillar and splayed side beams were all kept lime washed, as was the plastered underside of the slates.

Condensation and ventilation was no problem at any time of the year, but frost certainly was. Granfer's moustache freezing to the top sheet was not the only thing to freeze in the bedrooms.

All the bedrooms were distempered or colour washed which after a while began to flake off, revealing years of lime wash underneath. The rooms were entered from a long corridor stretching much of the length of the back of the house, lit by only one window at the head of the stairs.

Years later, my cousin Trevor was given a tricycle by Father Christmas, and being so excited when he woke, immediately rode it full pelt the length of the landing towards the bathroom, misjudged his turning to ride back again and rode straight down the stairs, crashing into the door at the bottom.

From Hacknell to Week

MOVING HOUSE

Moving our bits and pieces from Hacknell by tractor and trailer did not take long. We had very little furniture, little stock and few farm implements when we came to Week. Much the cheapest option for my father was to borrow his father's machinery; probably the only option, because very little farm machinery had been made throughout the war and then usually preference was given to those willing to do contract work for other farmers. Uncle Abie was ploughing for weeks every year with their yellow, Standard Fordson which had finally arrived in 1942. Grandfather having been on a waiting list for a tractor for a considerable time, the first available was accepted regardless of make or model. No self starters then: tractors were started – on petrol – by swinging the handle to turn the engine over. When running smoothly, fuel was switched from petrol to T.V.O. The registration number, FTA 264, I thought in my innocence stood for Fordson Tractor Association!

Almost certainly the plough was a two furrow trailing model and this, combined with the slow speeds of the tractor made ploughing a tedious business, though not as tiring as walking behind horses all day but much colder in the winter. Home Guard overcoats were put to good use by many farm workers. Abie made a cab of wood and canvas for the tractor – or it might have been John, his brother, who made it. This type of Fordson had a very slow bottom gear, ideal for driving along the stacks of corn at harvest time. The clutch on the wide platform was also the brake and could be held down with a hook when stationary. At eight years old I became a very willing tractor driver, between the rows of stacks at corn harvest. Being put in gear by the man who was pitching sheaves, I was able to operate the clutch/brake by standing on it and stepping off until the loading was complete. No Health & Safety inspectors in those days.

I think farmers who owned a tractor were still in a minority. John Watkins (Hayne) had a John Deere, on which Tom Buckingham learnt to drive. Dudley Hellyer owned an International Farmall, new in 1940, which Mrs. Bawden drove, the only lady I knew who could drive a tractor on the road at that time, little thinking that before many years had passed I would be doing the same and fifty years later still driving tractors. My daughters grew up expecting to progress from bicycle to tractors before they drove a car.

Cecil Crocker at Little Northcote Farm had a large Fordson Major which he used for almost full-time agricultural contract work from 1939. First in Burrington?

I remember when walking to school one morning from Hacknell, being given a lift by Mrs. Annie Mills (Lower Hacknell). This was fine until we met Cecil with his tractor and plough in the last long straight narrow part of Hacknell lane. Although having passed a wide place on the corner under the oak tree by only a few yards, she had no idea how to reverse the car, so Cecil had to reverse back to Red Post. Anyone with experience of doing this with a trailing plough will understand why I missed the bus that morning!

Farmers were able to hire tractors and machinery from the War Agricultural Executive Committee (WarAg). Again there were waiting lists, with strictly controlled time limits, so that the week or days the tractor was on your farm it was worked from dawn to dusk. Too bad if it poured with rain every day. My father hired a Fordson Major for one or two weeks and, apart from the hours of darkness, he and Bernie kept it working full time – well worth the £12 paid for the hire.

Mr. Pincombe was an elderly man when he retired and Week Farm was in a rather neglected state. Hedges which had not been trimmed for years were five or six yards wide. Seedling gorse and blackthorn suckers had grown up to meet the overhanging bushes, creating tunnels for sheep and bullocks to shelter behind but reducing the area of each field considerably – early type of "set aside"?

At Hacknell, each autumn two or three men spent weeks trimming hedges with hooks. walking through the middle of the hedge to trim the tops, but some were allowed to grow unchecked for a few years. These were "steeped" and the bank cast up during the winter, providing faggots and "hard" wood for the fires. Some long growth was laid to make a stock proof fence. Hooks had to be kept sharp, some men were more expert at wielding a whetstone than others. One casual worker was very crafty, he appeared so ham fisted that Ern Miller was cajoled into sharpening both their hooks while the other man had a rest!

As well as the hedges and land being neglected, the farm buildings were in need of much attention. The farmyard scenes in "All creatures great and small" are very similar to how Week was. At Hacknell doors hung straight and fastened securely; the tallet floors were sound enough to be a wonderful children's playground, one leading to the next, and to be a drying ground for wet washing on dismal days and smooth enough to brush up the eaver seeds before the new season's hay was brought in, but here things were far different. The tallets were so bad that two layers of wads of straw were never removed because that, plus the poles and gorse underneath them was all that kept one from falling into the shippons or bullocks' houses below.

"Wads" of straw are bundles, approximately 5 feet long, tied twice with binder twine at 1/3 and 2/3 of that length by the thresher. Loaded onto carts in the mowstead it was taken to the yard, one man pitching it into the tallets hole. It was easier if there were two men in the tallet, one to pitch it back to the other who built up the stack to the roof. This was called "packing it back" rather than "making the rick" when it was outdoors. The straw would be used for bedding or feeding mixed with hay if good enough.

Hay was cut out in squares from the ricks in the fields during the winter, loaded onto carts and dealt with in the same manner as the straw. How we loved to ride on the top of the load of hay, the sweet smell lingered until our hair and clothes were washed.

(A tallet is a loft in the roof space above a shippen or bullocks' house. Tallets hole – an opening in the wall which could be closed by a door or shutter when not in use).

The hay or straw was used as needed by pitching down into open racks (we pronounced this as RECK) against the wall or down into the "feeding paths" then up into the racks in front of the cows. Access for workers and children was either by ladders fixed to the wall at convenient places or by stone steps, outside at Hacknell but inside at Week. It was not unknown for a calf or sheep to go up these solid stone steps into the tallet. Going up was fine but many a tale could be told of getting them down again.

Free range hens – known to farmers as "Barns door fowls" were very partial to "stealing their nests" in the hay and straw, laying in the darkest corners, and maybe not discovered for months, until some unwary person stepped on the eggs, the resulting smell is one of the most unpleasant I have ever known. Even so it was a wonderful place for children to play, no present day dangers of bales toppling down.

Litters of kittens were also well hidden by their crafty mothers until weaning time, when they would be proudly displayed, and brought for their share of the twice-daily hand-milking feed time in the shippon below.

Col. Gracey spent a great deal of money improving and repairing the farm buildings but his enthusiasm was hampered by having to apply for building "permits" to obtain materials for Palfreman and Joint to use. Fred Chudley, the estate carpenter and Tom Friend (Bill's father) did the majority of door, window and tallet repairs and were with us for months. Reg Joint, Bill Bowden, Leslie Lewis, Fred Harris and others employed by Palfreman and Joint became familiar faces off and on during our first years at Week. Mum must have made hundreds of cups of tea to go with their packed meals.

WEEK

Aerial view of Week 1958

The house at Week was a complete contrast, being square with a wide front door leading into a good sized hallway, a sitting room either side and wide open stairs rising in three easy flights from the rear of the hall. Behind the right hand smaller sitting room is the dairy, cold on the warmest day with two windows, one facing north the other east. The larger room, once the kitchen, has a second door leading to the rest of the house; the same area may be reached by turning left at the base of the stairs into a smaller hall with a large walk-in larder opening off it. These areas were very dark until a glass panel was inserted into the front and internal kitchen doors. Whereas the rooms so far have been well lit and lofty, the kitchen and adjoining small scullery were low ceilinged and badly lit. Although twentytwo feet by nine feet, the kitchen seemed tiny compared with that at Hacknell.

This part of the house was originally the wash house cum back house with, we were told by Tom Friend, an underfloor well. When made into a kitchen, pig's houses directly outside the back door became the wash-house. At that time a door closed the opening into the garden wall leading to the front door, consequently, everyone came to the back door straight ahead. A gate replaced the garden door years ago but visitors still arrive at the back door.

The upstairs at Week is very nicely designed with the stairs rising to a galleried square landing, five bedrooms opening off this. Soon after we moved in, Mum painted the wood surrounding a square of lino on this landing. Being a notorious sleep walker I was warned not to step on the wet paint but following a trail of footprints on the twelve inch wide strip the next morning, the culprit was discovered still asleep, brown painted soles of feet gave the game away.

Back of the house before the lower roof was raised in 1951 to accommodate the bathroom. A branch of the large beech tree can be seen on the left. Middle and on the right, Nan and Charlie Wellington. On the left is Nan's sister Dorothy.

Ascending the stairs, after the second flight, the main stairs branched to the left but a shorter narrow flight branched right to a small low door leading into an attic room above the kitchen, only high enough for an adult to stand up where the sloping roof joined the main house. This room had been used to store apples in the Pincombes' time but seven years later became a bathroom and box-room after the roof was raised and doorway widened by digging away part of the cob wall. I well remember the mess, the fine greasy cob dust drifted all over the house, despite hanging curtains and blankets over doors. For some reason all the doorways, throughout the house and farm buildings are low. "Mind your head" is a constant warning.

Like Hacknell the kitchen was the most lived in room. Spars were made there on winter evenings, food was prepared, dishes washed and clothes were ironed on the scrubbed table and when re-decorating, the table provided a useful surface to trim and paste wallpaper.

Wallpaper at that time had a selvedge on both edges which had to be trimmed before hanging. I think we removed only one, the left hand side, which created flat ridges when hung. The alternative was to have little gaps showing because it was very difficult and tedious to cut the edges without notches. Later still the selvedge was perforated so that a sharp blow trimmed the tightly rolled paper. The wide ornate borders fashionable at that time also had to be trimmed by hand or the perforated wastage pulled away before being hung with a paste made from flour.

At Hacknell the greater part of farm buildings were thatched but here thatch had been removed years before, replaced by Bridgwater tiles, slates and galvanized iron.

Col. Gracey, although a dedicated preserver of trees, soon removed the large and ancient trees surrounding the house, some dangerously within a few yards. A huge beech only six feet from the dairy kept it cool but filled the gutters with leaves and mast in the autumn, branches lifting slates on windy days. Elm trees blocked the light from a small window at the end of the kitchen. Reg Murch helped to draw the trees with a traction engine and wire rope. Sawn up, they provided timber to repair the buildings and wood for our fires.

Coming home from school that first night I came into the only room I had seen before – the kitchen and saw my favourite cats, Nimmy, a long-haired tortoiseshell and white and Topsy, a black and white, sitting on the hard, black horsehair sofa making themselves at home. With those cats there, Week was my home then as well!

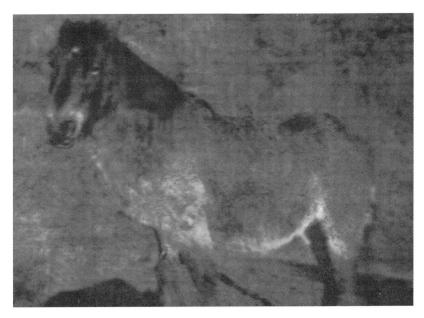

Queenie – over thirty years old

TRANSPORT

When we came to Week, car owners were still few and far between and those few cars were mostly of a low horsepower – 12 h.p. was considered a powerful car! Double de-clutching to change gear smoothly was a skill learnt easier by some than others, as was hand-signalling, for those cars without flip out direction indicators.

Throughout the war petrol had been severely rationed, so my grandfather's larger car was laid up for a few years, firstly at Hill Sampson in a shed that has now been incorporated into the house then in the "root" house at Hacknell where mangolds and flatpols were tipped to feed the cattle. What wonderful imaginary journeys we children travelled in that car and how useful the wide running boards were as seats for tea parties.

My father's Morris Minor – registration letters LJ . . . valued at £15 in March 1946 was like a square box on narrow wheels with a fold-up luggage carrier on the back. With no concession to passenger comfort, the back seat was a thinly padded board covered with rexine. Very little knee room separated this from the two front seats. When the engine was worn out, I remember going with my father in great uncle Albert's pony and trap to fetch a replacement from Dick Cudmore's scrap yard at Bridge Reeve, between Ashreigney and Chulmleigh. This pony, Queenie, lived to a great age, ending her days here at Week, a well loved favourite of our daughters. This little car continued to give valued service for several years after we came to Week until we had a bigger Morris – CAE 17 – in November 1950. During the war years, Dr.Wingfield drove an Austin 7. Those who knew him will remember what a tall man he was so he removed the driver's seat and drove from the back– made to measure!

For those without cars, Tom Wills' Tuesday and Friday bus, returning twice on Fridays was well supported.

Many farmers' wives, including Granny Eastman, had a stall – known as a sitting – in Barnstaple pannier market. These ladies would carry their produce in large wicker baskets. If there was not enough room inside the bus, the driver could climb a ladder on the outside to place baskets within rails on the bus roof. What an arm aching weight those baskets must have been by the time the women reached the market. Granny kept her stall near the corn exchange for a few years after we came to Week. Mum raised ducks and chicken, etc. to supply the stall but by then Granfer used to drive his car to Barnstaple on Fridays, parking in Prideaux or Brindleys for one shilling. This was much easier for granny than catching the bus. Liza Handford, of Court Mill, Langridge Ford – Granny's friend from the days they worked as housemaids at Hall, Bishopstawton – was only a little lady but she used to walk to Chapleton Station with two large baskets and then from Barnstaple station to the Market every Friday until quite elderly.

My family with grandparents George and Emily Hewitt

We sometimes used the train to visit my other grandparents at Braunton. I remember trains being many carriages long and very full, with people standing in the corridors. Many were airmen stationed at Chivenor or American and British soldiers from the army camp on the Saunton road – my first sight of dark skinned people. Often there

32

were one or two service men for tea at Granny Hewitt's, invited by Grandfather or one of my younger aunts. Sometimes the invitation extended to Hacknell on their day off.

At Braunton it was an easy walk from the station at Caen Street to North Down Road but after leaving the train at Portsmouth Arms we had a long, steep walk up through Northcote woods to Bewdown and Hacknell; to Week it was an even longer walk! By 1946 petrol was becoming easier to obtain although still rationed. Mr. Western was again selling from his pump by the oak tree. My Uncle Abie had a motorbike that our sheepdog Ben loved to ride as passenger, sitting on the tank between Abie's arms.

Young people considered it a step up in the world when able to buy a bicycle. Socials or dances in neighbouring villages, and Barnstaple on a Saturday afternoon became easier to visit. Not only the young rode bikes; for many older people it was their only means of transport. In fact, Mr. & Mrs. Bert Ellicott of Richards Cottage (now Bryher Cottage) shared a bicycle. To get to Burrington, for example, one would start at a fast walk, then the other cycled on ahead, left the bike in the hedge for the walker to then ride past the second person, so that they each walked and rode half the distance.

My first bicycle was a third or fourth hand, large wheeled "sit up and beg" sort, passed on from Edith, one of Mum's younger sisters, when I was twelve or thirteen. This had a cord threaded through holes in the mudguard to the centre of the wheel in the shape of a fan. This kept a lady's skirt from being caught in the spokes. Very few women wore trousers; even for work in the fields wearing trousers was considered rather daring! The Women's Land Army made them more acceptable wear, but even then some farmers' wives eyed these young women with suspicion!

This old bike was a real bone shaker but, oh!, the freedom and the pleasure of being able to cycle to Hacknell, to Burrington and to High Bickington on my own.

High Bickington

The Village, Burrington looking towards Chulmleigh

WATER AND SANITATION

What a step backwards in time when we came to Week from Hacknell. There we had hot and cold water indoors – the cold, gravity-fed from a reservoir below Hill Sampson meadow, the hot from a black cast-iron boiler standing at the side of the open fireplace in the middle of the back wall in the kitchen. An inefficient "Bakewell" formed the base of this open fireplace.

Unsuspecting thirsty children were invited to drink from the tube on a tap at the end of the house. Water came as a slow trickle at first then whoosh – their heads would go back as the downhill force of water hit them. Another trick was played when, with so many to use the bathroom while the evacuees were with us, sharing was the normal happening for the girls at least, then a sneaky pull on the chain from the high cistern gave a cold wet lift off to the victim sat on the toilet.

Drinking water came from the pump in the back kitchen, the source for this being a well beyond the orchard, cold and clear on the warmest day. A flush toilet adjoining the back porch and a bathroom with toilet and large airing cupboard upstairs was luxury indeed.

And when we came to Week? There was a pump over a stone trough outside the back door but because of leaks in the lead supply pipe this had not been used for a long time. Mr.Pincombe left the yoke he had used to carry water with two buckets at a time dipped from the well situated on the opposite side of the lane, below the house and farmyard. This well being only five feet deep, with no cover, was a great attraction to the dozens of Khaki Campbell ducks kept for egg laying. The stone trough is still in use but these days is filled with flowers by the garage, to brighten the entrance to the yard.

Our old pump trough

No water was wasted, a little went a long way and probably was used more than once. Hot water came from the large "Fountain" or a heavy kettle complete with "handymaid", hung on chimney crooks over the open fire; these had to be filled from the buckets of water. There was obviously no bathroom and the toilet was a draughty earth closet some distance away in the orchard – no roses around the door but several lilac bushes kept it shaded and buckets of ashes, sweet smelling.

Our toilet in the orchard, with Megan

Recycled newspaper is nothing new. The weekly paper was cut into squares, threaded with binder twine and hung on a nail in this stone building, no doubt re-read with frustration at the missing bits of interesting articles but "Never put off for tomorrow what you can do today" did not have the same compulsion at 11 o'clock on a dark, wet, winter's night!

Granny came to a sticky end in this fresh air closet when she paid a visit there the day after Mum painted the holed wooden bench, top and front. Paints were not quick drying in those days, at least not on the wood. On Granny's bottom was a different matter.

Liz Miller & Kate Huxstep

WASHING DAY

Washing day at Hacknell was comparatively easier than at Week, with a black cast-iron woodburning furnace in a corner of the back kitchen, trays of washing on the long form by the kitchen table in front of a large window and with hot and cold water at the shallow sink on the opposite side of the room. Liz Miller from Kingsland, the workman's wife, used to help Mum and Gran on washing day and at Week, Mrs. Emily Smith helped mum. She lived in Week Cottage with her retired husband, Percy, daughter Rosalie and son-in-law, Arthur Parkhouse, our workman.

Fifty years ago wash day was a mammoth task wherever it was, without machines to help, when working clothes were sturdy and thick and sheets were made of heavy white twill.

Because the kitchen at Week was so dark, on dry days the washing took place on the cobbled area outside the back door. Water was heated in a large 10 – 15 gallon boiler hung over the open fire to wash the clothes, then re-filled with shredded bar soap added to boil the whites. Wringing, rinsing several times, blueing, starching, putting through the mangle followed – the only concession to making the task easier – before hanging on the line using gypsies' clothes-pegs or spreading on a low hedge to dry. Soapy water from the boiler was not thrown away until after it had been used to scrub the kitchen floors, or maybe scour the outsides of calf-feeding buckets, etc.

Beds had to be remade with clean sheets after the feather "tie" had been turned and relaid over the flock mattress or straw palliasse (commonly called "pollyass"). Meals still had to arrive on the table at the usual time – cold meat, pickles and boiled potatoes, with apple-pie for mid-day. Calves and poultry to be fed, cows milked, morning and afternoon, eggs picked up and cleaned, between dealing with the drying washing. On a blowy day starched garments were brought in slightly damp and rolled up before being ready to iron.

I soon learnt that a wet day was not the best time to ask any favours. I still remember howling at the pain and indignation of being tapped with the washing stick wielded by granny. This was a smooth, stout stick to lift washing out of the furnace boiler.

Ironing of almost all the clothes except towels was with a relay of flat irons heated against the glowing coals of the open fire. The clothes were then spread on a clothes-horse in the kitchen to air thoroughly. It was regarded as quite dangerous to wear "doney" (damp) garments – as bad for you as sitting on damp ground!

What did they do in the evening? There were always socks to darn or mending to do before bedtime – and that was only Monday's work!

Any old irons?

WEDDINGS

Weddings were far different from the often very elaborate occasions fifty years on.

*Wedding picture of John and Beattie and
bridesmaids, Margaret and Freda*

My uncle, John Eastman, married Beatrice Parkhouse of Fox Meadow at Burrington Church on the 29th September, 1946. Precious clothing coupons were used for wedding outfits, so something suitable to be worn many times as "Sunday best" was usually chosen. Beattie wore a pretty long-sleeved, pale blue, knee-length dress, with navy hat and shoes. Her bridesmaids, myself and school friend, Freda Parkhouse (Beattie's sister), wore shiny, pink satin dresses; again knee length, but with short puffed sleeves and headbands of pink feather flowers and satin bows. White ankle socks and sturdy brown lace-up shoes (our only shoes) completed the outfit. Mrs. Alice Phillips of Balls Corner made the bridesmaids' dresses. No doubt some brides were able to borrow or buy a white dress but I think those for Beattie's wedding were typical of country farming weddings.

Except for royalty, wedding rehearsals were not thought essential preparation for the smooth running of this important day, so. . . after the marriage ceremony when the bride and groom walked up to the altar, then knelt for the vicar's blessing, Freda and I followed suit kneeling right behind them!

There were no visiting photographers in 1946. So, a trip to Barnstaple a few weeks later by the bride, groom and bridesmaids is the only record of the event. Even if any guest had a camera, film was virtually unobtainable to non-professional photographers during and for some time after the war.

No such thing as printed invitations; guests were invited in person or by letter because telephones were few and far between. Northcote Manor and Burrington village were the nearest to us. At the time all calls were connected by an operator through a manual switchboard.

As was usual then, the "self-catering" reception was held in someone's home – in this case at Hacknell, having larger rooms than Fox Meadow. I think we all managed to sit at the big farmhouse table, probably twenty to twenty-five people. Only immediate family plus Aunts and Uncles would have been asked. Weddings were much smaller affairs then and never an evening party as well. (Do we hear some fathers sighing for the "good old days"?).

I remember Freda and I singing "on yonder hill there stands a creature; who she is I do not know ...." with its chorus of "Oh, no John, no John, no John, no!" at some time during the reception. I also remember the top tier of the wedding cake collapsed onto the floor, earlier in the morning. It was a case of "what the eye doesn't see..." and sticky syrup to the rescue.

Wedding present lists were still very much in the future. Brides were grateful for any gifts, no colour schemes or patterns of china and cutlery were suggested then!

Beattie carried a bouquet and we bridesmaids a small round posy, in something like a silver paper doily. The only flowers in the church would have been the normal two altar vases – as far as I can remember.

And honeymoons? Yes, honeymoons were "in" by then but usually only with a friend or relative, at a suitable distance away – at least the next parish! Newly weds were the victims of many good-natured practical jokes such as making an apple-pie bed, etc. to embarrass them. Easy to arrange if they honeymooned fairly locally but John and Beattie went with Aunt Florrie and Uncle Bill to London! The Seychelles, Tunisia and the Caribbean were a long way ahead in more ways than one.

I had been to only one wedding before John and Beattie's, that of Mum's younger sister Muriel to Alan Brailey at Braunton with the reception in a neighbour's sitting room, and three others including Bernie's to Phyllis Kingdon at Burrington with the wedding breakfast provided by Mrs. Elworthy at Upcott before my own marriage to Eric in 1956. Having Mrs.Webber cater for the forty six guests at 10/- a head and a white dress for myself, home made at £2 10s. 0d, was certainly a first in our family.

*Bernie & Phyllis
at their wedding in 1950*

Our wedding,
15th September, 1956

Our Ruby Wedding,
15th September, 1996

CHILDHOOD AND SCHOOL

The only memory of my first day at school in 1940 was of being driven by my father to the village, then Mum taking me in to be registered – before leaving me there – and that was that! It is unlikely I had ever been inside the school before then; suddenly I was there full time, in surroundings which had been familiar to my maternal grandmother, Emily née Webber of Curzeland. In her childhood it was an all age school, the infants' classroom with tiered seating being converted to boys' and girls' cloakrooms before my schooldays and altered yet again, into the school office by the time my grandchildren spent their infant and junior years in the same building.

When we moved to Week, school continued without a break except that I caught Wills' bus at the top of Week lane instead of at Red Post, to arrive in plenty of time at Burrington School – after having had to walk the whole distance when the evacuees going to Chulmleigh more than filled the bus. A local High Bickington boy, Eric Bolt, was a passenger on that bus. Little did I know that ten years later we would be married.

The senior classroom in the main building was in the area that is now used for mealtimes. A black "tortoise" stove with an iron guard rail was against the corridor wall so only the children sitting in the row of double desks at the very front felt any warmth; even that was hindered by the fact that Miss Gillies usually stood, leaning her elbow on the rail as she taught the whole class – with her hat and coat on when it was very cold! Many children suffered from chilblains on their hands and feet and would have suffered more if Mrs. Dallyn's mother, Mrs. Heal, had not taken pity on those who came to school wet through; she often dried our coats and even dressed us in some-thing of Myrtle's while our clothes were drying in the school house.

Miss Cissie Jury, the infant teacher, will be remembered by her pupils for her quick temper. She also taught sewing, where her idea of instilling knowledge into our heads was by several sharp taps with her thimble – very painful – so when redness began to spread up her neck to her face, we kept our heads down. The only thing I remember making in the sewing class was a pair of knickers from a stiff, salmon pink, cotton material using "A pattern for a pair of pilch knickers". They were so long in the making, stitching run and fell seams by hand that they were outgrown long before finished.

We were taught to be very miserly with paper during the war, writing small and neat to the outer edges of the exercise books and leaving no margins. We made paper chains at Christmas by glueing interlocking coloured strips or concertina folding three to four inch strips of crepe paper, then cutting the edges into a pattern, repeated the full length when opened out. We made hanging Japanese lanterns one year. These were not as welcome to decorate our homes as the chains were; anything Japanese brought to mind the atrocities carried out in their camps on prisoners of war.

I had piano lessons after class one afternoon a week with Miss Jury, so during that summer term, having missed the bus, I walked 2$\frac{1}{2}$ miles from Burrington back to Week, very seldom meeting a car on the way. I think the walk did me more good than the music lessons!

Mum, Dad and I walked to Week from Hacknell on a Sunday afternoon a few weeks before we came here to live, so that Mum could agree a price with Mrs. Pincombe for any furniture, curtains and lino she wished to leave. She was also shown Hilda Pincombe's wedding dress and the red velvet bridesmaids' dresses. I was left in the kitchen with Mr. Pincombe, who sat on a seat inside the open fireplace, and did not even see the rest of the house until I came home from school the day we moved in. Can anyone imagine a child today sitting still, not examining their new home or seeing someone's wedding clothes with their mother? I still feel disgruntled about it fifty years on!

CALLERS AT WEEK

I am not sure if it was because petrol was more readily available, or because Week has a much shorter lane with three dwellings visible from the road through to Burrington, from Week Cross to Colleton Mill, whilst Hacknell is almost 3/4 mile from Red Post. Whatever the reason, we seemed to have many more callers at Week. At Hacknell we had a weekly butcher, Reg Slee; twice weekly baker, Edie Owen (formerly Percy Turner's Bakery) and monthly grocer, Goodings – all from High Bickington. My grandparents, having farmed at Shutley, High Bickington, before moving to Hacknell in 1932, had kept their links with traders there. Various reps. for animal medicine firms called. I can remember at least six, all very persuasive, all having the best universal cure-all.

These came in bottles, boxes or drums with paper instruction labels which rapidly became eaten by insects or unstuck and fell off, so that after a while it was uncertain if contents should be mixed with water, sprinkled on feed, given as a drench, or rubbed in! Fortunes were made by those firms from what farmers eventually threw away! Berry's, Bibby's and W.C.A. reps. took orders for animal feeds to supplement the main home-produced, corn, flatpolls, mangolds, swedes, turnips and chaffed straw. Pickards supplied grass seed mixtures and some of the root seeds, but I also remember Dunns and Garton's "travellers" (reps) coming.

Our only newspapers were ordered at Mr. Wallis's by the "Red Petticoat" café off Butcher's Row and brought home by Granny on Fridays. The "Knockout" comic for me and Farmer & Stockbreeder and Picture Post magazines were eagerly awaited.

An occasional gypsy called but that was about it, except at flatpoll pulling time when many farmers came for plants. Flatpolls are cattle cabbage, now an almost unheard of and ungrown cattle fodder crop.

Seed was sown in August, usually after wheat had been harvested, the seedling plants grew through the winter until they were pulled individually by hand in April, counted in twenty-fives, bundled in hundreds and sold by the thousand, to other farmers to be planted as an autumn and winter crop. Planted at the rate of seven thousand to the acre, they produced a heavy crop most years, depending on the weather.

From start to finish flatpolls were a very labour-intensive crop which had to be cut and loaded by hand every few days, brought to the root house, tipped out, then loaded into a wheelbarrow twice a day to feed cows and other cattle.

When we came to Week we seemed to be over-run with callers. Gypsies came every few weeks, the Sanders and Penfold families had many relatives. I think Mum was probably too kind to them – we had many yards of elastic – stretched! and combs! Before soft plastic or nylon combs, we had very brittle ones which broke easily; if one tooth came off, the rest soon followed! Mr. & Mrs. Orchard from Colleton Mill called twice a year – flashing their gold-filled teeth as they showed their stock of aprons, towels, pillowcases, etc. Clothing coupons were needed as well as money.

Squires at Torrington called fortnightly to exchange the wet battery for the wireless (radio). At Hacknell, Mr. Ern Webber recharged the batteries.

Eggs were collected weekly by Ern Venner at Week and by Mr.Wilcox at Hacknell. Reg Slee began to call twice a week with meat, Routcliffe's bakery from Chulmleigh delivered twice a week as well as Edie Owen. Tom Moore, South Molton, brought calor gas and paraffin, Venners came monthly with ironmongery, etc. Twinings Tea had a rep. who called six-monthly. On answering the door, he had a regular opening phrase "Twinings famous teas – something for everybody ha-ha-ha"! A lady came from Exeter annually to buy bags of feathers – after Christmas poultry picking. "Jimmy" Singh came monthly with his suitcase strapped to his bicycle. He was the first we knew with nylon stockings to sell.

48

Miss Blake from Tawstock called twice-yearly with underclothes, such as liberty bodices, directoire knickers, etc. She was also a Spirella corsetier, supplying made-to-measure corsets, for these were still the days of a firmly controlled figure no matter how small or large.

Every week it seemed brought an animal medicine or seed firm salesman and insurance agents were most persistent as always, Bill Richards called for Pearl Assurance and Ron Birchall for Prudential.

We had regular visits from the Agricultural machinery firms we had seen at Hacknell. Fertiliser and lime merchants all had their salesmen; later on, when we had a tractor, oil reps. came regularly. Many of these men were ex-service men.

Goodings continued to take orders monthly on a Monday and deliver groceries the next day, giving a month's credit. Tom Hill, from Butcher's Row, called every week selling fish and fruit with Ern Turner, Mum's cousin, to help him. Years later Ern's daughter, Christine, married Mowbray Webber formerly of the Barnstaple Inn, Burrington.

Many of these callers went away time after time without an order or sale; some were a nuisance, others we were pleased to see. One who was always welcome was Miss Annie Smith who went all around the parish, twice a year, to collect for "Waifs and Strays" and the "Zenna Field Mission". To do this end of the parish she returned from Barnstaple on Wills' bus as far as Week Park Cross, then collecting from the houses at this end, she would have tea with us before continuing her journey. Later, when I had passed my driving test, I drove her to outlying farms, before taking her to her home at Winswood. Annie liked to have an idea of how much money was in her tin before it was officially counted so I was instructed to "try to see how much they put in"!

When we came to Week, although still Burrington Parish, our postal address became High Bickington. Alf Lemon and his dog walked the post round – through Snape, Gratleigh, Kingford Hill,

Week, Deptford, etc. and all the places either side of that route. We had our post at 8.30 a.m. in those days.

Papers were delivered daily, left in a pipe at the end of our lane by Lorna Snell who was soon replaced by demobbed airman, Bob Mellows, who had taken over the round. Forty-three years later he sold the business – we knew he wouldn't last!

There must be others I have forgotten but it is easy to understand how news travelled fifty years ago – without the benefit of T.V., radio or telephone.

The Square, Burrington with old oak tree

WEATHER IN 1946

1946 was memorable as being one of the wettest autumns on record. Two fields I remember being grown to corn that year at Week were between the house and Kingford Hill, facing north; the worst aspect possible for a wet summer.

First ploughed in 1946. The same cornfields in 1947

With great difficulty the corn had been cut with horse and binder, the sheaves stacked – or stooked, depending whereabouts in the county you were born – and left, as usual, two or three weeks to dry out before carting to the mowstead (rickyard). It rained day after day, the sheaves were sodden and had to be re-stacked several times when there was enough wind to dry the outside – this then became the inside. Really wet sheaves were opened and spread on the ground to dry, but, before this was complete, down came the rain again. I am not sure if any had been ricked before John and Beatie's wedding on September 29th but certainly the majority was harvested in October.

Following this frustrating autumn, was a severe winter, with deep snow for weeks on end, drifts against the hedges froze so solid that sheep could walk anywhere, in our own or our neighbours' fields, over the tops of the hedges. Thankfully, we had no problems with frozen pipes in the house and farm buildings, one consolation of not having plumbing!

Every drop of water had to be dipped from the well by bucket, wet hands freezing to the handle of the bucket on contact. From the well to the house was some distance, across the lane to the top of the yard. My father, wearing nail boots, leather leggings and a thick khaki army greatcoat, slipped on the ice-covered yard while carrying two pails hitched onto Mr. Pincombe's wooden yoke, spilling the water over himself. The coat was frozen so stiff by the time he reached the house, that when taken off, it stood up by itself!

Although lambing in March in those days, the freezing conditions continued through lambing time. With no sheds to house the sheep, they had to lamb outdoors. Unless someone was on the spot, to lay the newborn lamb on a hessian bag, they froze to the ground very quickly and died.

At some time freezing rain fell coating every twig and branch with a thick layer of clear, shining ice, the slightest breeze setting up a tinkling as of a thousand wind chimes. With an orchard adjoining the house we had very disturbed but musical nights, something to take your mind off the coldness of a visit to the free-standing, stone-walled toilet in that orchard.

Many trees were damaged, the weight of ice splitting off branches. Telephone wires collapsed under the strain – the whole telephone system in rural areas was above ground at that time.

By some means we had a message to say there would be a quantity of bread at Portsmouth Arms the next day. Dad, Bernie and other neighbouring men walked – or rather floundered – through the snow to bring home as many loaves as they could carry in clean hessian bags.

Salt pork and potatoes must have been a large part of the diet for weeks, with other vegetables frozen in the ground and the butcher unable to reach us. I am sure Mum would have had a good stock of basic groceries in the larder at that time of year and there were plenty of eggs freezing and bursting their shells as soon as they were laid. That winter was an experience – but not to be repeated too often. Say, once in a lifetime!

At the time few farmers in North Devon grew barley as a single crop, it was usually mixed with black and/or white oats, sown as "dredge corn" making a balanced feed for cattle in winter.

Today dredge corn is an unheard of crop because with combines came the need for all the grain to be ripe on the day of harvesting, whereas when binders were used the corn was cut slightly under ripe, then ripened in the stack. Oats and wheat were grown as single species – oats to feed the horses, wheat to provide reed for thatching, the grain sold to merchants and millers, depending on quality – providing much needed extra income.

Snow at Week.
The lane was filled to the top
of the hedges in 1947.

Hazel, Kathleen, and Elizabeth Paul
at Dole Park Lane February 1978

Week Cross, February 1978

FOOD

There was little change in the food we ate after leaving Hacknell because Mum had done much of the cooking there and food, by necessity, had to be seasonal; the usual way of preserving meat and runner beans was by salting, fruit was bottled or made into jam.

Coming from Hacknell with its two high ceilinged, well-lit, large square kitchens, to the long, low kitchen at Week with a small scullery at one end, must have made preparing and cooking food difficult for Mum. Small windows and brown gloss paint half-way up the walls to match the smoke -blackened ceiling from a continually smoking open fire, when the wind was any direction but southerly, added to those difficulties. Another hazard was the enormous number of crickets who lived between the stones in the chimney, coming out mostly at night, their loud chirping was company on a quiet winter's evening, but their sudden hops often surprised us for the adults were quite large – about $1^{1/2}"$ long, plus legs!

At Hacknell we had large gardens with a plentiful supply of fruit and veg, but at Week only a small area was in cultivation until Dad cleared the brambles and stinging nettles from the rest of our dark-soiled old garden. Runner beans have been grown in exactly the same position every year since 1946 but other crops in rotation. No doubt in that first year we enjoyed the produce from Hacknell.

Apples were an important part of our diet and discovering which varieties were growing in the three orchards at Week was quite exciting or disappointing, depending on flavour! Apples in tarts, dumplings and stewed with custard and cream were almost year-round sweets, but other things were very seasonal, such as lamb tail pie in the Spring.

After being cut off, the tails were baked in the oven to a stage where the wool could be plucked off, before being jointed and made into a rich pie of bones and jelly. My interest in this delicacy disappeared with the plucking, long before the eating, but half-grown rabbits, jointed and fried with a seasoned breadcrumb coating, still make my mouth water!

Fish had to be brought home from Barnstaple. Rabbits and poultry cooked in many ways were a regular change from salt pork but whatever home-produced meat was used meant work for the women. Rabbits had to be skinned, poultry plucked and drawn, pigs' meat salted down, etc. etc. – almost a holiday to have the butcher call once or twice a week with tripe, lamb, beef or sausages!

Real clotted cream was always available, yesterday's milk, poured into a large pan left undisturbed for twenty four hours for the cream to rise, scalded today for tomorrow's cream; nutty flavoured, scalded milk for use in tea and as a refreshing drink on its own. Calves and pigs had the surplus.

We almost never had breakfast cereals. I can only remember Cornflakes being occasionally available – imagine the cost for a family of eight, or more! Our usual breakfast was bread and cream with syrup or home-produced honey and jam. Ten o'clock (lunch time) was either fried eggs, bacon and potatoes or cold meat and pickles, again all home-produced. 1.00 p.m. (dinner time), the main course plus a sweet of whatever fruit was in season or rice pudding. Junket was on offer at some time most days, rennet being bought in quart bottles. 6.00 p.m. (tea time) – bread and cream or butter, cakes, savoury flan, scones, yeast buns, pasty, etc. All except the bread were home-made in our household and having to pack lunch and dinner for five each schoolday and for Dad all year, cooking was a constant chore. No list of the food we ate would be complete without mention of "Teddy" cakes – potato cakes to non locals – these were a regular standby for tea. The mixture was shaped into $2\frac{1}{2}"$ rounds, approximately 1" thick which were fried in a 14" pan hung over the open fire. We children were like sniffer dogs homing in on the source of the mouthwatering aroma. Each in turn would go into the kitchen, returning with a teddy cake for all, by the fourth or fifth time we were full! The recipe, with all amounts approximate, is:

8 ozs. flour	1lb. mashed potatoes
2 – 4 ozs. dried fruit	2 – 4 ozs. sugar
2 eggs	4 – 6 ozs. fat

Mix together, roll into balls with floured hands then flatten. Fry or bake in a hot oven.

I still have the large frying pan Mum used then, hung as decoration in the sitting room open fireplace.

Fireplace with frying pan

Fifty years on, thank goodness for freezers, fridges and well-stocked shops!

Kathleen Gracey's wedding

Children attending Kathleen Gracey's wedding, 1937

*1. Freda Short 2. Mary Cooke 3. Doreen Headon 4. Joyce Snell 5. May Western
6. Maureen Headon 7. Gwennie Snell 8. Amy Western 9. Mabel Madge
10. Hilda Baker 11. Walter Smith 12. Hilda Palfreyman 13. Ivor Parkhouse
14. Jack Davey 15. Michael Davey-Harris 16. Margaret Eastman 17. Brenda Parkhouse
18. Cecil Hellyer 19. Vera Madge 20. Rita Easterbrook 21. Herbert Tancock*

CLOTHING

Although fashions in clothes had altered considerably in the fifty years leading up to 1946, notably the length of female skirts, there can be no comparisons to the last fifty, with skirts of any length and trousers normal wear for women and girls.

I well remember wearing hard brown leather sandals in the corn-fields, chasing rabbits and how the razor-sharp stubble of corn cut with a binder, dug into my ankles making them bleed, how painful this became when I was given a bed-time wash, no way would I have washed my sore legs myself. Socks needed clothing coupons and darning, so summer was a time for saving on both.

Winter time – knee-high grey or fawn socks were worn when it was very cold, but I cannot remember anyone at Burrington school, boy or girl, or older girls attending Chulmleigh Senior School, wearing long trousers, even at home. We all suffered cold, red knees and, if legs were plump, very sore, chaffed thighs, especially when walking in snow. Even having longer elasticated knicker legs was no help; they soon became wet and cold rubbing sore legs ever more painful, so we walked as if we had lost our horse until the skin became hardened or we got used to the pain!

In the early 1940s new shoes for growing children were very difficult to come by, so any hand-me-downs, however badly worn, found a welcome home – by the grown ups at least!

One such "passed on" at Hacknell was a pair of hobnailed boots – I was assured that they were girls' – and despite strong protests, was made to wear them to school. But only once! I can still remember the teasing for being the only girl in boots – some boys still wore them. I have forgotten what I wore the next day, but it was not boots!

Fifty odd years on, how things have changed; now my grandchildrens' great desire is to wear a pair of Doc. Martins' boots! Clumpy lace ups, but without hobnails. One young lady – who I won't name – wore them with a dark green bridesmaid's dress at her Aunt's wedding party!

Can anyone else remember the machine at Tucker's Shoe Shop in Barnstaple? This was an X-ray Machine to see if shoes fitted – every pair that was tried on! The dangers of over-exposure to radiation were obviously not realised in those days.

Most girls wore "liberty" bodices and wool vests, often hand knitted, keeping bodies warm in winter; these were replaced by cotton locknit in summer, worn no matter how hot the sun shone. Virtually all cardigans, jumpers, pullovers and socks, even swimsuits, were hand knitted. Women were seldom without a garment on their knitting needles. I cannot remember ever choosing my own clothes before we came to Week. Clothes were either made for me, passed on from relatives, or very occasionally brought home by Granny or Mum from Barnstaple to try on; then being changed the next Friday if they did not fit. There was usually plenty of allowance for growing!

I loved one handed-down dress from Mum's younger sisters which almost certainly had been passed on to them, for Granny had difficulty enough stretching their income to feed and buy essential clothing for the family, without buying frilly dresses.

It was pink figured satin with a fitted bodice, puffed sleeves, gathered skirt with a short flounce around the hem and – this was the special part – five or six frills in the shape of horse-shoes on the skirt.

My mother, father and me
(in that pink dress)

60

Ethel Tucker who had lived at Hill Sampson with Mrs. Rippon before they moved to Howards Cottage in High Bickington, made a skirt for me from the good parts of one of hers, the material unpicked and turned inside out. This was made without a waistband or fastening, joined to a white cotton vest top; a simple to make and easy to put on style. To wear over this top she knitted a striped jumper, using up odd bits of wool of all colours. I can remember proudly wearing this for the first time to show Granfer. I still think of his comment whenever I meet someone wearing stripes – "You're like a carrot half scraped"!

For ladies, new clothes would usually be bought for a special occasion and almost always included a hat, relegating previous best, worn to Church etc., to "second best," worn to Barnstaple, visiting the family or friends; still with its matching hat, these in turn became "working clothes" to be patched and washed until threadbare.

For men, hobnailed heavy leather boots were worn all year round, with stout leather leggings in wet weather. Put on in the morning before going outdoors, they were unlikely to be removed before bedtime, for it was a time-consuming task, not like slipping your feet into Wellingtons. No wonder farmhouse floors were uncovered by carpet or even lino. A long handled, hard brush kept by the backdoor was used to clean off the worst of the mud or dung. Plenty remained to be deposited on the cemented floors at Hacknell and Week, swept up daily, but much waited for the vigorous scrub on hands and knees using the soapy water remaining after the weekly Monday wash.

And for the men, again a new suit began as best clothes, sending the rest in turn one step further down the scale; it is a long time since I have seen a farmer wearing his old suit for work in the summer, or hessian bags tied around his waist or draped over his shoulders to keep dry during heavy rain. No such things as waterproofs or a Barbour jacket then. Wellington boots were available, but were scarce and expensive and unable to be repaired at the local cobblers.

Thick Oxford shirts, corduroy breeches or trousers were Autumn-through-to-Spring wear; waistcoats were worn all the year round – necessary for the pockets, to carry a watch, a piece of whet stone to sharpen knives, nails and for all the other odds and ends farmers carry in their pockets; and for smokers, their baccy tin, for many smoked heavily at that time, evident by contemporary photos. Snuff taking was also quite common then.

To save washing thick working clothes too often, men would use their pocket knife to scrape off thick wet mud, and rub out the rest when dry. I was reminded of this recently when I took a tumble at Fursdon Farm Sale and Roy Ley came to the rescue with his knife, thank you Roy!

I cannot remember seeing any man working outdoors without his shirt, or wearing shorts, before we came to Week. Bob Mellows, delivering papers daily, and a man collecting eggs weekly, were the first – and the only men for many years whom I knew to wear shorts when it was very hot. I would think almost every man wore braces to keep up his trousers. Some wore a wide leather belt as well. "Builders' bottoms" were never visible.

Women at work were never without an apron, either a flowery cotton crossover, pinafore or bib and brace, with a coarse or "towser apern" over these for dirty work. In the evenings, a waist apron might replace these. Nylon stockings were very new and precious in the late 1940s; so hard to come by that little repair shops opened to mend nylons at so much a ladder. I remember one in Joy Street, Barnstaple, where a girl sat inside a window with her machine, doing repairs while customers waited outside in the street. As nylons became more readily available these shops quickly disappeared.

With a large family and shortage of clothes, there was always mending to be done, sheets to be turned "sides to middle" or some smaller garment made from something old. Granny's hand sewing machine did sterling service down through the years, but especially during the war.

When Granny was fifteen and working at Honiton rectory she had saved enough money to buy a longed for bicycle. Her eldest sister, Eliza Gulley lived at Exeter, so offered to buy it for Granny, but bought a Singer sewing machine instead, reasoning that it would be more use than a bike. At fifteen Granny did not see it that way!

Hair styles were mostly plain and simple, many women wearing their hair in a roll on the nape of the neck. Both grandmothers and my mother wore this style in the 1940s. Either a piece of tape was tied around the head and the hair rolled into that, or the hair was rolled and secured with hair pins or grips. Over this a fine hair net was worn. Fifty years on, a few ladies still wear their hair dressed in this manner – tidy and economical – for they never need to spend money on cuts, sets or perms.

My father used to cut my hair, just a straight, ear-length bob – I remember it being ear-length from the time he nipped one with his scissors and the amount of blood that flowed!

He cut hair for many men and boys making a small charge for this service. Few in the country went to "town" barbers then; most villages and communities had a local self-taught man, with varying degrees of barbering skills carried out sitting on a stool or chopping block in the "back house" or shed. My father took a pride in his work, but some amateur barbers sent their customers home well shaved up, not needing to come again for several months.

Most men, when outdoors, wore a hat or cap of some kind, winter and summer. Caps, like other garments, went down the sartorial scale as they became older, from "tidy", fit for market, to "home about" for work: useful for holding down barbed wire, pulling brambles off sheep, as a container for mushrooms or eggs, for kneeling on in a muddy field to deliver a new born lamb, etc.etc., and for throwing at an inattentive dog.

MR. A. EASTMAN

Sympathy is extended to Mrs. A. Eastman and family of Hacknell Farm, Burrington, in the death of Mr A. Eastman after a short illness. Deceased was greatly respected as was seen by the large attendance at the funeral on Thursday at the parish church.

The mourners were: The widow; Mr. and Mrs. George Eastman Mr. and Mrs. A. Eastman, Mr. and Mrs. J. Eastman, Mr. B. Eastman, sons and daughters-in-law; Mrs. E. Parker, sister; Mr. and Mrs. C. Eastman, brother and sister-in-law; Mr. W. Smith (representing Mrs. Clatworthy, sister); Mr. and Mrs. W. T. Pearce, brother-in-law and sister-in-law; Mr. A. Way, brother-in-law; Mr. and Mrs. W. Friend, Mr. and Mrs. J. Farley Mr. and Mrs. W. Eastman, Mr. and Mrs. W. Heal, Mr. and Mrs. C. Heal, Mrs. G. Morrish, Mrs. W. Eastman, Mr. and Mrs. W. Eastman, nieces and nephews; Mr. J. Laythorn, Mr. A. Eastman, Mrs. J. Pall, Mr. W. Eastman, cousins.

Floral tributes were sent as follows: "Fondest love of dear dad," his sorrowing wife and children; "In loving memory of my dear brother," Charlie and Bess; "In loving memory of a dear brother," Lizzie, Alice and Albert; "To dear grand-dad," Margaret and Norman; "In loving memory of dear Bertie," Florrie and Bill; "In loving memory of dear Uncle Bert," Winnie, Bessie and Walter; "In affectionate remembrance of dear Uncle Bert," Jack and Edie; "With sincerest sympathy," Colonel and Mrs. Gracey; "In loving memory," Bill and Trix; "In loving memory of a dear friend," Tilly, Edie and Fred; "Deepest sympathy," friends at Winkleigh; "With deep sympathy," Mr. and Mrs. Frank Cater; "With deep sympathy," Mr. and Mrs. E. Miller; "Deepest sympathy," Mr. and Mrs. Watkins and Shirley; "With deep sympathy," E. and F. Elworthy; "Deepest sympathy," Kate "With deepest sympathy," Mr. and Mrs. W. Mills; "Deepest sympathy," Bert and family (Kingford); "Deepest sympathy," Mr. and Mrs. Mountford (London); "Deepest sympathy," Mr. and Mrs. W. Rippin; "Sincere sympathy," Grace and Maurice Seage; "Deep sympathy," Mr. and Mrs. Hewitt and family

Funeral report and announcement of my father's death

Funeral card

IN EVER LOVING MEMORY

OF A DEAR HUSBAND AND FATHER

ALBERT EASTMAN

of Hacknell, Burrington

Who passed peacefully away,

On Monday, February 23rd, 1948,

AGED 62 YEARS

A light is from our household gone,
A voice we loved is still'd
A place is vacant at our hearth,
Which never can be filled.

Interment in Burrington churchyard,

Thursday, February 26th at 2.30 p.m.

A GRAVE BUSINESS

Although not attending a funeral until I was seventeen or eighteen, I remember older members of our family going, dressed in very sombre clothes. My father and grandfather wore dark suits and black bowler hats. My father continued to wear his possibly to the early 1950s (I still have it stored away). Ladies would not dream of going to a funeral without a black hat and black gloves, even if their outfit was grey. Grey had been considered "half" mourning, to be worn towards the end of the usual six months.

On second-best clothes, black armbands or a black diamond of material stitched on the upper arm of a jacket were worn by men and boys for months afterwards, possibly never removed to reveal the faded patch.

Black-edged memorial cards were still being sent, able to be printed, posted and received in time for relatives and friends to come to the funeral. I remember addressing those for my grandfather at Hacknell in February, 1948. The undertakers for his funeral were Murch Brothers, the agricultural engineers at Umberleigh – many forget this was ever part of their business.

Newspapers carried full accounts of all the mourners, relationship to the deceased, those unable to attend, the floral tributes with the message on each one, and an obituary supplied by the local correspondent. Service sheets, donations in lieu of flowers were not usual, if at all at that time, but a sit down cold meat meal for the family before the funeral was.

I have been told that at my great-grandmother's funeral in 1935 Aunt Poll, her daughter from near Newton Abbot, brought a cooked joint of beef for the meal at Hacknell. Unfortunately, our dog fancied it, taking it out into the farmyard. Quickly recovered and washed off discreetly, not wishing to waste good food, the unsuspecting

Aunt Poll, her husband and son were served generous portions of beef and the remainder wrapped up for her to take home for their next day's dinner. I never had the impression that Granny and Aunt Poll had a close sisterly relationship even before that.

My great-grandparents,
George and Mary Way
of Rags Cottage, Warkleigh.
He was accidently drowned,
aged 69, crossing the river Taw;
she died, aged 90, at Hacknell.

Crowds attended the Sunday afternoon Armistice service at Rock Park in Barnstaple. Bands played and ex-service men paraded, resplendent with medals – Granfer Hewitt was one of the many – we took him back to Braunton afterwards. I think this was 1946 but may have been earlier or later. On November 11th at 11.00 a.m. all traffic stopped for two minutes; the volume of vehicles was far different then, but drivers were willing to pay respect to their fallen countrymen.

My maternal grandmother was the last person I knew to have her clothes ready for her "laying out", several years before her death. She had a large white, fine cotton, nightdress with hand-crotcheted lace collar and cuffs and other items needed, neatly folded in a piece of material. This was in the late 1950s. She led me to believe that this was quite a common practice years ago when it was a matter of honour to be prepared for death. Insurance policies were paid at one or two pence a week to cover future funeral expenses up to at least the 1950s. Memories of the workhouse and being buried "on the Parish" were as real and near in time to that generation as 1946 is to me.

Granny and Granfer Hewitt

My great grandfather's funeral card

CHILDHOOD TREATS

Children's treats and birthday parties of fifty years ago seem very tame by today's standards. No "theme" parties, Macdonalds, swimming at Cascades, "sleep-overs", hired videos or take-home party bags then.

Usually we had to walk to wherever the birthday was being celebrated. Hazel Wedlake's at Churchlands was quite a step from Hacknell, 3¹⁄₂ miles, at least. Hazel met us in the village at a certain time. It is amazing how arrangements were made without the benefit of telephones and with the children not possessing watches. (Christmas 1946 was the first time I knew of a child being given her own watch). I cannot ever remember being worried if one of the group were late arriving, presumably we were sent off from home in plenty of time and excitement gave our feet wings.

Leaving the village on the road towards Chulmleigh as far as Bircham Farm, we continued through the yard to a cart-track leading to Churchlands. This short cut took longer than expected, because on the way we passed by derelict cottages at Southwood, which we obviously had to explore, from the outside only. The back wall of the cob-built houses had fallen out exposing the interior and staircase on the north side. I remember being quite envious of Hazel having a ruined cottage to form a background for all kinds of imaginary adventure stories and journeys. (I believe the houses were on Bircham land).

A birthday party at Hazel's I remember well was a picnic by the river Taw, just upstream from Kingsnympton station – South Molton Road in those days.

On the Burrington side is a wide shelving gravel "beach" where we could safely paddle in the shallow water – extremely cold in the shadow of trees even on a hot summer's day. The railway is very close on the opposite bank and I remember steam trains pulling in and out of the station and the passengers waving to us while we were paddling and picnicking on the bank. Walking from Hacknell to Burrington, then to Churchlands before reaching the river and returning by the same route, was no doubt regarded as a "treat" by me, with the picnic and paddle an extra bonus.

Tea was always the highlight of a party; It was amazing what some mothers – and at Churchlands, sisters Joyce and Audrey – produced, despite most foods being rationed in the 1940s. Wobbly jellies and trifles were rare treats and carefully portioned out, but today's luxury, a large bowl of home produced clotted cream, was always on the table.

At many parties we just played school playground games or explored the farm buildings. At Christine Hellyer's party at Twitchen we did a really exciting and dangerous thing! We all climbed up a ladder into the tallet (loft) to peer down through the hayrack to the Red Ruby Devon bull below, until Dudley, Christine's father, shooed us out. The way to Lower Twitchen in those days was diagonally across the Hellyers' yard to a narrow rocky lane, so steep that we children seemed to be looking down on Mr. & Mrs. Cole's roof.

At Hill, Barbara Babbage's mother organised a more traditional party, with games such as "Pass the Parcel", "Hunt the thimble", Hide and seek", "Blind man's buff" and even "Postman's knock"! We had running games in the massive dairy taking care not to fall down the steps to the cellar at the far end, where I think apples were stored – definitely not cider.

Mr.Babbage did a circular trip with his car to the village, picking me up at Red Post on the return journey, the car full to overflowing with children by then.

The first peacock feathers I ever saw were in a vase on the mantlepiece at Hill. I thought they were beautiful – I still do – but when I told my family they were horrified. I was told how unlucky it was to have those feathers indoors; on a par with bringing in Box bush greenery, May blossom, and hearing a lone robin squeaking.

70

At Averil Tancock's home, The Barton, we played "hide and seek" – all over the house! In one bedroom was a kidney-shaped dressing table with a floor-length flounce. A wonderful place to hide, something I had never seen before, but for years it was my ambition to have one!

Shirley Watkins' parties at Hayne were memorable for me because Mrs. Watkins drove their car – the only mother who did so while I was at Burrington School.

At Hacknell, my birthday being in January, I only remember summer parties, no presents, just friends from my year at school; Barbara, Hazel, Christine and Barbara Cowley (Brock) plus younger Shirley Watkins, Ann Rippon and Freda Parkhouse. Raymond Mayne, a Bristol evacuee, and Mowberry Webber made up the seven of our class.

We played around and inside the buildings, played with the cats, followed tracks in the woods and had tea around the big kitchen table. I hope all those now 'over 60s' remember those simple childhood gatherings with as much pleasure as I do.

Not a treat as such, but in the days when we made our own amusements, Oak Apple day, May 29th, was celebrated each year at school by picking stinging nettles and trying to sting each others' bare legs; holding up a sprig of oak leaves was supposed to give immunity, but a fat chance of that when your back was turned.

A winter treat was to find an ice slide. A field at Hacknell facing Lower Hacknell had a gutter across the slope which overflowed when there was hard frost. The resulting ice slide down to the bottom hedge gave hours of fun, small doors being hauled from the farm yard to provide a seat to hurtle down the hill. That at least was the theory, more often than not we parted company after a few yards, but cold numb legs, hands and bottoms, barely felt the grazes inflicted on them.

Burrington Fair was another eagerly awaited season. We always had the Monday off school I'm not sure about Tuesday which then was sports in the afternoon, public tea, followed by adults' races.

Burrington Fair, when held in the Square

On Fair Monday our men, or at least some of them, went to the cattle sale in the Square, usually with stock to sell. Women and children did not go from Hacknell, so I have no memories of that until I was much older, but I know it was traditionally a day to invite friends for lunch after the Fair. It was 1946 or 1947 that I first remember the swing boats and hoopla on the Green with stalls on the playground; the day ended with the Fair Dance, dancing led by a real live band.

Another Fair eagerly awaited was that at Barnstaple in 1946. The first after being discontinued, I believe, for the duration of the war. We went on the Friday evening by Wills' bus, being dropped off near the Albert clock in the Square. The Fair was on North Walk in those days, stretching from the Queen Anne statue to Mermaid Cross. The claustrophobic, narrow entrances funnelled the tightly packed crowd into the wide central area past lots of small stalls, such as hoopla, coconut shies, darts, rifle shooting and leading past the "cheap jacks" with their continuous line of amusing sales talk and onto the big rides, helter skelter and side shows. One such I recall with discomfort was the Freak Show exhibiting the fattest Man and Lady, sat on chairs inside a roped off area; the public were able to view and comment on, their ample proportions clad in brief, shiny, satin outfits, from all sides

I remember the excitement – and fear – of being part of such a crowd, a new experience for me. Saturday was carnival night with a few of the smaller stalls in the pannier market. I remember nothing of the carnival but recall clearly meeting Mum's cousin in the High Street and him telling us that ice-cream was on sale at the Ice Cream Parlour – Devito's – the first since war time. So we joined the queue for my very first taste – delicious!

Socials were a popular fund raising event, a mixture of games and dancing suitable for families of all ages. Whist drives were well supported, especially the ones with Christmas poultry for prizes. The local hunts and political parties ran qualifying whist drives, where the winners from a winter-long series of local evenings played off at the final, usually for sizeable monetary prizes.

However small the event, it almost always concluded by the audience rising to their feet to sing the National Anthem.

Cousins
left to right:
Brian Hewitt, Maureen Jenkins,
Anne Hewitt,
Jean Pugsley and Rodney Jenkins

When we came to Week on the Western edge of the Parish, 2½ miles from Hacknell and the village, visits from school friends were less frequent owing to the extra distance to walk. However, we were not without visitors that summer; there was a constant stream of younger cousins, with or without their mothers, Mum's younger sisters. Eastman cousins, Norman, Jean, Trevor, Robert, Valerie and David were yet to be born. My mother and father were the eldest children of their respective families so I had an uncle, Bernie, and aunt, Evelyn, only six years older than me.

Despite the very wet summer we had a whale of a time, exploring the buildings, the fields, the woods and the remains of an old cottage towards Kingford Hill. These ruins were only two walls about four feet high, no staircase or upper storey in those ruins, but a carpet of snowdrops the next spring where the garden had been. Many years later we discovered from the 1840 tithe map that it had been called Bakes Cottage, with Wood Green nearby.

At Hacknell, the Jewells at Hill Sampson and the Mills at Lower Hacknell were our nearest neighbours, both at some distance. At Week we had Mr. & Mrs Bob Underhill and their son Bill at Higher Week, with Mr. & Mrs.Percy Smith, their daughter Rosalie and son-in-law Arthur Parkhouse at Week Cottage, all within shouting distance. What with Mr. & Mrs. Jefferies at Mitchells (now Bryony), Mr. & Mrs. Cecil Squire at Week Park and Mr. & Mrs. Reg Murch and daughter, Deanne, at Week Cross, compared with Hacknell it was thickly populated!

Then in September, for the seven children in my class at Burrington School how our lives changed! We began secondary education in five different schools. From having Miss Gillies as our sole junior teacher and Miss Jury for the infants, we had more teachers than there were children at Burrington School.

A winter treat for many years was Mrs. Gracey's Christmas Party, possibly in the Hall before it burnt down in November, 1944. Some I can remember being in school on an afternoon before the end of term, and visited by Father Christmas who gave each child a beautifully wrapped present from under the tree.

An earlier article about Mrs. Gracey's Christmas parties revived memories for Cecil Crocker. It was his task each year to transport the tree from Northcote Manor to the school by horse and cart, escorted by the two estate carpenters. After setting up the tree, they found it necessary to visit the Barnstaple Inn across the road to quench their thirst, but not Cecil, he had to stay with the horse and wait – and wait!

Another party was at her home, Northcote Manor. I am not sure if that was a school or tenants' children's party but I do remember the thick swags of intertwined greenery hung corner-to-corner across the kitchen ceiling just like those seen in Victorian books.

Mrs. Gracey also gave presents to the tenants' wives and children – so I had two presents – buying and wrapping them herself, she sent their groom, Gerald Cann, in the pony and jingle to deliver them locally. When petrol rationing eased, Leslie Brownscombe, the recently demobbed chauffeur, took over this task, their previous chauffeur, Charlie Wellington who had married the Gracey children's nanny, had to leave at the outbreak of war, to be employed in a munitions factory at Bristol.

Mrs. Gracey gave me a doll one Christmas with closing eyes and fair wavy hair. Calling it Mary, it joined my other dolls, Joan and Peter, in the woven rush clothes basket which had been my cradle when a baby. I am not sure why one was called Peter for it had none of the necessary attributes, but in my innocence I thought his face looked like a boy's!

Some time after the war ended, instead of a party, Mrs. Gracey hired Tom Wills' bus from Atherington to take the children, including those at senior schools, to the pantomime at the Theatre Royal, Exeter. What a treat! The costumes, the music, the dancing, the colours and lighting effects were just magical for us children; most of us had never seen anything like it before.

Fifty years on I am not sure if we went to the evening performance or the matinee, but I do remember what we had for tea. Each child was given a paper bag containing a thick slice of marzipan-topped slab cake, a large sausage roll and some kind of fancy cake all supplied by Routcliffe's Bakery, Chulmleigh. I have no idea what we had to drink; the ring-pull can had not been invented then, so it would have been a small bottle or beaker filled from a larger container.

For the next few years Granny Eastman took me to the Exeter Pantomime, booking and travelling with Wills' coaches. Every year the scenery was more spectacular than the previous year. Once, there was an amazing waterfall, almost the complete width of the back of the stage, changing colours, with the lights shining through the falling waters. The scene only lasted a short while but the memories live on.

At Christmas 1946, presents were, as usual, few and simple. I was given a pink cotton nightdress with a patterned bodice and a pair of slippers by Mum and Dad, a blue mottled-case fountain pen from Gran and Granfer Hewitt, writing paper and envelopes from Auntie Cissie – one of Mum's six sisters. I cannot remember what I was given by Granny and Granfer Eastman, probably something to wear, but I do remember the make of pen – it was "De la Rue". Having had one term of French lessons from Mademoiselle at Crediton High School, I could translate it as "of the street" – possibly the only reason I can still recall my presents for that Christmas and not for many others. Without the prompting of present day television, radio and advertising from September to December promoting the toy/game/clothes/shoes etc. of the year, I think we were all pleased with whatever gifts we were given.

Looking back to that time of post-war shortages, beginning farming on our own at Week, clothing coupons, and the need to purchase quite an extensive and expensive school uniform for me, I now appreciate how difficult it must have been for Mum and Dad.

*Summer uniform at
Crediton High School.
Pat Ayre, my fellow outboarder,
on the right, 1949.*

Granny Eastman provided a brown leather school satchel from Jim Gubb, a saddler in Boutport Street, Barnstaple and, thanks to some minor repairs by Mr. Jim Western, it was still in good condition after five years continual use and is still useful fifty years on to carry clippers and sprays for trimming and treating sheeps' feet. Autograph albums were still very popular then, being passed around to family, friends and teachers. I still have mine which I made in craft lessons, but there is no comparison with a great Aunt's which has exquisite watercolours and pen and ink drawings.

My one and only ride on a tricycle was when sent to post a letter at Northcote Cross at eight or nine years old. I passed the crossway without finding the post box and had almost reached Northcote Lodge when I met Mrs. Jim Harris out for a walk with her young son, Ken on his tricycle. She re-directed me back to Northcote Cross – known as Donkey's Lodge in those days – and there was the post box – a large brown box inside the garden hedge (Mr. & Mrs.Willis' garden today).

Col.Gracey had a private and presumably paid-for arrangement with the Post Office to collect parcels and letters from this box. Local people also made use of the facility to save walking to Burrington.

Before retracing my steps, Mrs.Harris asked if I would like a ride on Ken's tricycle. (I thought she would never ask!) I remember Ken as being very reluctant to give up his seat, but I was more than eager to take advantage of the unexpected offer and this made it well worth the one and a half mile walk from Hacknell.

Another treat for me was an occasional visit to Barnstaple with Kate Huxstep, the cook and a former Nanny at Northcote Manor, long-term friend of Mum from the days when she was a kitchen maid there. We usually paid a visit to the cinema, where the programme then was continuous so that, if one wished, British Movietone or Pathe News, adverts, main and supporting film could be joined at any time or the whole programme be seen through twice. Tea at Bromley's was Kate's treat for herself after shopping was completed, going in the ornate High Street entrance somewhere opposite the former National Trust shop. The waitress, in black dress, white fancy apron and white headband, came to take the order which for Kate never varied, always a large plate of bread and butter, cut wafer thin and evenly spread right to the edges. A mixture of fancies was ordered for me. I believe the charge was for each cake eaten, so the more we ate, the more we paid. I have been told that one lady was especially skilled at cutting bread and butter and always cut as and when it was ordered – no cling-wrap then!

By High Bickington Church Hall, the day the bus shelter was opened.
Left to right: Margaret Eastman (now Bolt), Rose Eastman, Maud Eastman,
Kate Huxstep, Bert Eastman

THE SCHEDULE referred to

No.on Ord.Map	Name	Cultivation	Area	No.on Ord.Map	Name	Cultivation	Area
594.	Cottage & garden.	Cottage	.936	561	Kitchen Park	Pasture	2.225
562.	Buildings & MowPlot	Buildings	1.337	550.	Road Park	Arable	6.655
563.	Orchard	Orchard	1.516	555.	Sand Park	Arable	3.231
566.	Roadway	Roadway	2.of2	598.	Sand Park	Arable	3.259
602.	Meadow	Pasture	1.107	632.	Ridge Lands	Arable	4.945
601.	Meadow	Pasture	3.365	630.	Bew Down	Pasture	3.549
626.	Longland Orchard	ARABLE	.806	628.	Broad Park	ARABLE	3.515
652/570.	Longland	Arable	3.879	631.	Long Meadow	Arable	.545
	Parks	Pasture	3.831	648.	Lucas Park	Arable	5.208
571.	Hallams	Pasture	.347	651.	Broad Park	Arable	3.611
567.	Hallams	Pasture	.645	650.	Three Corner Field	Arable	
568.	Hallams	Rough	.428	649.	Long Field	Arable	4.49
659.	Mr. Broom Hill	Arable	4.362	709.	Marshlade	Pasture	.804
661.	Old Quarry & Wood	Wood	1.225	647.	Moor Close	Arable	4.350
623.	Wood	Wood	.765	711.	Moor	Rough Pasture	2.537
624.	Lower Broomhill	Arable	6.441	708.	Little Marsh	Pasture	2.552
544.	Lower Wood	Arable	3.346	706.	,, ,,	Lady Field ARABLE	3.194
542.	Plot & garden	Pasture	.662	705.	Crest ,,	Arable	4.040
549.	Cleeve	Brake & Rough		707.	Roadway	Roadway	.198
549.		Pasture	5.123	59.	Pt.WeekDown	Arable	.949
565.	Higher Down	Arable	4.996			A.	106.189

X. 628 and 651 Run together 16.

592: Hallams - Coombe Pasture
16.603 do
60.4 do

Part of tenancy agreement 1946

NATURE RAMBLINGS

Having fewer distractions, we children were possibly more aware of seasonal changes and the wildlife and nature around us. Returning from school took much longer during the annual summer feast of wild strawberries – we remembered every patch from Hacknell to Burrington from previous years.

We ate "bread 'n cheese" – wood sorrell with its pale green clover shaped leaves and "zour zabs", another sorrell with dark green pointed spade-shaped leaves, both sharp flavoured but thirst quenching on a hot day. We gathered nuts by the pocketful to be eaten fresh or stored for a winter treat. Fifty years on, being able to crack nuts with my teeth is a sadly lost pleasure; fillings, crowns and expensive dental treatment have put a stop to that joy!

At New Buildings – now "Gone with the Wind" – gooseberries grew on the road hedge, temptingly hanging down at children's height. They proved irresistible to Raymond Mayne, a Bristol evacuee who lived at Hill Sampson, and me. Maybe they were a small cultivated variety; certainly by the 1940s the wildest thing about them were Mr. & Mrs .Parkhouse (Bill and Em) when they realised what we were doing! The next evening's scrumped fruit were spat out faster than they went in our mouths. Gooseberries sprayed with paraffin are uneatable and undesirable!

Wild gooseberries grew, and still grow, in several hedges at Week. Sloes and bullace were eaten in small quantities when fully ripe, the astringent mouth-drying effect probably similar to cheap wine! Weeks of blackberries took us to late autumn, with its ever shorter days. Hacknell was reached much earlier then, with the hooting of owls for company. Beyond Lower Hacknell, beside the cart track leading down to the stream and woods, grew wild raspberries in profusion. All this wild free food my mother called

GRAUNGE (I can only guess how it is spelt). Come mealtimes and no eagerness for food, I well remember Mum saying "You have been eating too much graunge". The unpredictable early autumn crop of field mushrooms and the later horse mushrooms were always eaten cooked – never raw. No other fungi were eaten; all others were regarded with suspicion.

And here is a timely warning of the dangers of eating unknown fungi from the 1928 diary of Miss Kathleen Joslin, then of Boutchland Farm – kindly loaned to me by her son, Norman Dennis:-

On August 14th Aunt Polly Dillon of Pavington (Mrs. Joslin's sister) came to tea at Boutchland but by the 16th she was very ill. Two doctors came. Ern Webber came for Mrs. Joslin and a stream of relatives were with her day and night.

As well as Joslins, Percy, Herbert and Bessie Babbage are mentioned – Mrs. Dillon was Polly Babbage from Ley Farm. The following are some of the daily entries:

On 21st – Auntie Bessie and I washed eight sheets
On 29th – Aunt Polly fell out over bed

Then she began to recover:

September 1st Auntie is heaps better, it is only weakness now. They have a girl now (domestic servant). *Aunt Polly has been very, very ill – all through eating mushrooms*

Daily visits continued until September 8th.

In the summer, cows at Hacknell were grazed during the day in fields between Hill Sampson and Kingsland and it was the task of the older children to bring in the cows on the way home from school. We began calling "Culp, culp, culp" soon after leaving the bus at Red Post, so they were waiting by the gate when we reached Hill Sampson. Eventually as the eldest – and only – child this became my task.

The much shorter lane at Week, with bushes arching over it like a dark green tunnel gave less scope for foraging than Hacknell's long lane with many of those hedges given an autumn trim over with paring hooks before the days of mechanical hedge trimmers.

A new discovery at Week was English Field Maple – one of the oldest of our native trees, distinctive by its yellow autumnal colours and bright red young growth in the spring, on trimmed hedgerow specimens.

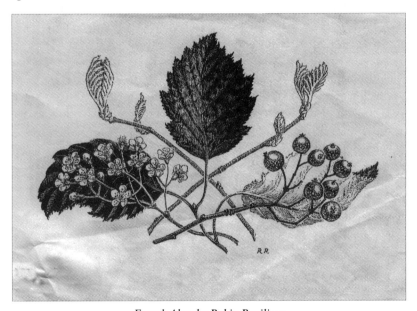

French Ales, by Robin Ravilious

Another small sized tree new to me but known by my father and Uncles, was French Ales, a member of the whitebeam family, local to this area – Sorbus Devoniensis – easily spotted in spring with its upfolded leaves downy white on the underside, before opening flat to show the dark green waxy upper surface. Growing to the size and shape of a medium sized apple tree, the bunches of white blossom in the spring produce small round fruit, like miniature Russett apples in autumn. These are edible when "bletted" – almost rotting – then made into pies, but there is so little flavour I cannot imagine why anyone bothered to do so when there was such a variety and quantity of local apples.

Wych Elm, with larger leaves than English Elm and pretty lime green blossom, and Spindlewood with orange berries inside a bright pink calyx, a gourmet meal for pheasants, I had not seen at Hacknell – maybe I overlooked them.

Red squirrels were common at Hacknell and at Week, a delight to watch leaping through the trees or scampering along the ground, but sadly soon to be replaced by the more aggressive rat-like grey ones. Before coming to Week I had never seen a badger – as far as I know there were no earths at Hacknell, the nearest being in the woods towards Boutchland, and at Week the nearest earths were at Gratleigh. Now they are widespread, in woods and hedges and some fields becoming undermined.

Foxes were seldom seen by day. Hen houses were taken to the cornfield errishes after harvest, for the hens to feed on any corn left behind and to scratch out germinating weeds. Shut in their house at night for safety, there were seldom any problems in daylight. Now foxes killing hens right up to the windows of our house, have forced us to abandon free-range hens for those kept in wire netting pens, with weld mesh laid flat on the ground around the house to prevent a repetition of badger and fox tunnelling underneath during the night.

Hares were plentiful at Hacknell with only an occasional, possibly annual, meet of the beagles to disturb them, they were often to be seen, when walking along Hacknell Lane, in Mr. Crocker's field by Hamlyn's Moor (2nd on the left from Red Post with a wire fence). In Spring they leapt and gambolled round and round, stopping to rise up on their haunches for a session of shadow-boxing. Mad as a March hare is an apt description! No hares were to be found at Week then, but swarms of rabbits, even more than at Hacknell, eating what little grass was here.

Although weasel, stoat and fitch all did their part to keep the population down, a constant battle was waged against rabbits in those pre-myximatosis days by whatever means possible. Ferrets were reared and trained to bolt them from their holes to be shot by waiting "guns". Wire snares and gin traps were used routinely and, I must say without too much thought for the cruelty aspect, for controlling rabbits could be the difference between being able to pay the rent or not and most landlords required their tenant to control pests in tenancy agreements.

Moles were trapped in the spring by small traps set in the runs and, if there was a serious problem with damage to grassland, strychnine could be bought – I think a permit had to be obtained – and the poison register signed.

At Hacknell we had a large pure white neutered tom cat – Bonzo – who was an expert rabbit catcher. The edge of his ears would be black-rimmed with cat fleas easily seen in the white fur. He would travel quite some distance when hunting rabbits, as far as Bill Rippin's at Ley, Lower Hacknell and Northcote. He would bring his catch to eat at home, before sleeping it off for much of the day. He was a very tidy cat, for after eating all the animal except the skin, feet and paunch, he lifted the coir mat in the front porch and tucked all this offal underneath. Not the pleasantest of footfalls for the unsuspecting.

Bonzo was a very intelligent cat for he had discovered how to open the back door; wide and heavy, this door was fastened by an iron latch. Sitting on the old fashioned mangle, kept in the open back porch for convenience on washdays, he could just reach the latch when fully stretched. After several trial attempts of rattling the latch and judging the distance accurately, he would launch himself off the mangle so his weight would force the latch down far enough to lift the lever on the inside allowing the door to swing open and give free access for whatever dogs and cats were waiting on the step. A visitor to Hacknell invariably announced his presence by rattling the latch just like Bonzo; sometimes one was mistaken for the other. One day

Granny hearing the latch being shaken called out as usual "Come on in Mr.Halway" and he did! Not Bonzo that time.

Cats occasionally got caught in gin traps sometimes when trying to steal an easy meal before the trapper checked his traps morning and evening. Soon after we came to Week, my pet cat Nimmy was caught in a trap set to catch rats. I was frantic. I couldn't keep her still to spring the trap. Dad and Bernie were away from the farm yard, so I ran the short distance to Higher Week and between sobs told Bob Underhill, Bill's father, of my plight. He soon solved the problem by holding down the cat with a hay pick, he was able to release the trap with his foot. After a few days Nimmy was none the worse, but I was never allowed to forget the panic I was in by "old" Mr.Underhill. Now I realise how relative age is when I pass the tombstone erected to him and his wife, Primrose, in Burrington churchyard – they were both in their early fifties when they died: he in 1948 from heart problems; she in 1953 after being an invalid, suffering from rheumatoid arthritis for most of her married life. Their son Bill then became the third generation of tenants at Higher Week.

Bernie had a very tame ferret called Bill, who was let out each evening to run beside him as he shut in the hens, then, back at the hutch, would run up his trouser leg into the hutch for a bread and milk supper. When Bernie made a new hutch for his ferrets, he was taking great pride in cutting a round hole between sleeping quarters and run, his father suggested that it would be quicker to cut a square hole. "Have you ever seen a square ferret?" was the swift reply.

Pheasants and partridges were commonplace at Hacknell having been reared in large pens in Moory Made (Mead?) up to the Second World War for Colonel Gracey. The game shooting was reserved by him and tenants forbidden to do so by a condition of their tenancy.

Slow worms basking in the afternoon sun in Hacknell Lane some-times found themselves in our lunch boxes to be released when we had shown the adults, but often forgotten by the time we reached home, until we heard Mum screaming when packing our meals the next morning.

Although owls were often to be seen at Hacknell, at Week, they roosted and reared their young on the top of cob walls in the tallets, a new experience for me. I thought the owlets were dying when I watched them regurgitate large pellets of waste.

I cannot remember anyone collecting birds' eggs at Burrington School but we had a great interest in finding and identifying nests. I can still recall a wren's nest underneath the thatch above the tallet steps at Hacknell, bluetits in a crevice in the wall and chaffinch in a fir tree out in the Mowstead. Swallows each year rebuilt dozens of nests under the eaves of the stone barn roof at Week. Then, as now, the nesting pair would have twittering arguments about the site of their nest! None now nest under those eaves, the smaller number who return nest inside the buildings.

Kathleen feeding her lamb at Week

Haymaking at 'Rags' Warkleigh

HAYMAKING

Being a child in the forties I remember the fun of haymaking: the long, hot summer days – extra long because of double summer time, (clocks put forward two hours in the Spring). The wet days, the seriousness of being so dependant on the weather – the sheer hard work and shortage of man power escaped me.

Hay turners were small and primitive compared with today's high-tech models. When the hay was deemed to be fit after several days, it was raked by a man riding on a seat above the horse rake; holding reins to guide the horse harnessed in the shafts with one hand, and working a long lever in the other. The tail of the rake was raised at intervals to deposit the gathered hay into straight rows across the field.

Next came the horse-drawn hay sweep – like a huge, wooden comb laid flat on the ground, attached to the horse with chains, the back supported two large handles an arm's width apart. Guiding the horse along the rows of hay, a man walked behind the sweep holding these handles – and the reins – until the sweep was full. Then, pulling out from the row, walked to where the rick was to be made, in the same field obviously: the "mow bed" of hedge parings, topped with straw as a dry base for the rick, having been made previously. The handles were lifted to overturn the sweep, so emptying the contents. This was a skilled job, and hard work when repeated all day.

The hay was then pitched with a "pick" (a two-pronged fork) onto the rick where one or two men, depending on its size, made the rick (another skilled job). They spread the hay evenly over the whole area, keeping the middle full where the men stood and gradually getting wider as well as higher, so that the sides sloped into the base and, therefore, shed water easier.

At some point it was judged time to start roofing in. I am still amazed that a man could decide by how much hay he could see left in the field, the right amount needed to make the roof – too little and the roof would not have enough pitch to shed the rain and too much could be an embarrassment with a steep, top-heavy roof and still cart-loads left and be the butt of every neighbouring farmers' jokes!

The sides of the rick were raked firmly downward with a handrake, again to shed water. I think these rakings were pitched up on the rick along with those from the field. The whole field would have been raked over again by a man and horse. Every bit was precious and needed for winter feed. Some farmers even fixed the hay sweep to the front of their car, just reversing to leave the heap by the rick, much easier than having to tip the sweep.

The rick was then thatched, sometimes by a local thatcher, some-times by a farm worker skilled in that craft. "John Willie" Webber did those at Hacknell, before my Uncle Abie became proficient at thatching. Probably a thatcher was employed early in the season to leave an extra man to help with the next field. I am sure older farmers/farm workers will be able to tell me.

When the hay rick was made, came the anxious time of the rick heating up, necessary for good hay, but not overheating and bursting into flames. If over-heating was suspected, or the rick began to twist in shape, long iron bars were driven into the rick and left there, checked at intervals for the degree of heat. Sometimes they were too hot to touch and this was a crucial time. Various remedies could be tried, such as cutting out a narrow section through the hottest part or using an implement called a hayborer to make a hole in the rick – anything to try to reduce the heat. To my knowledge we have never had a rick burn, but some hay was very brown, what was known as yetted (heated) hay. At Hacknell a hay pole was bought in 1942 or 1943. This made haymaking much easier.

The process in the field was the same, but the hay pole erected by the side of the rick supported a large grab which was dropped wide open onto the pile of hay, then the jaws pushed together to engage a slip catch. It was then raised and lowered by a horse being led forward to raise and backwards to lower the grab – sometimes my job when older. Controlled by a rope held by the man on the ground, the grab could be swung over the rick and then a sharp tug released the hay within reach of the rickmaker. As time went on, tractors were used instead of horses.

However, not everyone in our family was pleased with the purchase of this "modern" invention. Granfer and Granny Eastman were away for a couple of weeks nursing Granny's brother in south Devon through a terminal illness. His eldest sons, my father George, Abie and John, having tried to sell Granfer the labour and time-saving merits of a hay pole for a few seasons, seized their chance during his absence. Finding the hay pole in use on his return he was in a "right old tare" (cross) and told his sons that "laziness wouldn't get them anywhere"! Soon superceded by balers, I wonder how many hay poles were recycled by being used to pipe water underneath a gateway?

In those days, and for many years after we came to Week, hay was the only grass crop – for most people at least. There was not the option of making silage or big bales. Soon after we came to Week, balers were beginning to be used in Burrington, at first stationary, then pick-up balers. I remember a conversation between my father and Jim Pincombe at Abbotsmarsh at about this time. Dad said that hedge trimmers were here to stay but he thought the balers would end up in the river, because so much hay would be spoilt by being baled too soon. We bought a stationary baler for £300 in 1952 and our first Welgar pick-up baler two or three years after that – he had been soon converted! Bernard, his youngest brother, baled many acres for neighbouring farmers in the Burrington and High Bickington area as well as our own hay. With increased noisy mechanization, gone were the days of good humoured conversation whilst working, the companionship of sitting down together in the field, enjoying food from a large cloth-lined basket, provided by the famers' womenfolk. The basket needed to be large for the hearty appetites of the men, and for us children, food from the basket was twice as desirable as the same food on a plate. The dogs soon learnt how to sit looking appealing for the remnants.

This basket of food was called by various names, depending on the time of day. "lunch time drinking" at 10 a.m., "dinner" at 1 p.m., and just "drinking" in the afternoon. Tea, hot or cold, was carried in big enamel milk cans and, of course, home-made cider was provided in heavy stone jars, kept in the shade and refilled as often as needed from the barrels in the cider house at Hacknell and barn at Week. Other farms may have been different but that is how it was for us. Gone also are the days of making the hay "sweet" for young men who, with a roll of hay – one of many left by the sweep sliding over the ground – to wrap around the neck of the farmer's daughter or any young woman helper, claimed a kiss to "sweeten the hay".

After the rick had settled down, it was thatched with a thin covering of reed – enough to make it waterproof until the time came to begin using the hay. To fix the reed to the roof of the rick, spars and straw ropes were used.

My grandfather made all the straw ropes by hand, using a simple gadget called a "wink". Spiked into a post of the cart linney at both Hacknell and Week at working height for him, and with a good supply of straw beside him, he kept up a steady rhythm of adding straw to the tail of rope coming off the spinning wink. An easy looking task but much harder than it looked. On winter evenings spars were made, indoors by the open fire. Hazel sticks, approximately two inches thick and four feet long, were cut earlier, to be split lengthways into quarters, each end sharpened, before twisting firmly in the centre and folding the two ends so the finished spar looks like a giant hair pin. Packed in bundles and stored until needed, hundreds would have to be made each winter to replace broken ones. The kitchens at Hacknell and Week were easily swept clear of the chips of wood afterwards, no doubt adding fuel to the fire. Sometimes the twisted tops were tarred to be more weatherproof. Not having a supply of spars from previous years, Dad had to buy hundreds in his first year at Week. He paid Reg Murch £5 in October 1946 for spars at 2/- a bundle – of 50?

CHRISTMAS

The Christmas after we came to Week and all my earlier ones at Hacknell are remembered, partly for rabbitting parties for the men in the daytime, followed by card parties in the evening, but mainly for poultry picking and feathers!

For my mother it was the end of many months of hard work and a multitude of problems, rearing geese, turkeys, ducks and chicken to reach their peak of growth and fatness at Christmas. From the time of the stock-breeding birds laying their eggs in the Spring and these "sittings" of eggs being put under broody hens of old fashioned heavy breeds such as Rhode Island Reds and Light Sussex (taking the eggs away from them every day kept the stock birds laying), through the anxious time of hatching, when the young could be trampled by the hen, or stick to the inside of the shell and need dampness to help them to break free, it was a worry – that is always presuming that the eggs are fertile, that rats have not eaten them, that the hen has not gone off her broodiness and let the eggs get cold so the chicks died in their shells.

Mum, on the right, with two "paying guests" and some of her laying hens. Newly enclosed mowstead in the background.

93

The number of eggs in a sitting and the precise number of days before hatching, varies with each breed. After hatching, each brood stayed with their hen foster mother, in separate coops, being free to roam by day as they became older. Then as well as danger from rats, sparrow and buzzard hawks were sometimes a problem and, for ducks, a condition called "sprawls" was a serious concern caused by strong sunshine on their backs before feathers gave an insulating cover.

Feeding was carefully adjusted, from a diet for healthy early growth, containing chopped eggs, finely shredded greens, dandelions and stinging nettles with meal, to one with boiled potatoes squashed into wet meal, known as "mix meat" to fatten them. As the birds became more mature, fights would break out between the stroppy young turkey males, sometimes to the death, but usually with some damage caused by sharp beaks and talons.

Despite all these setbacks my mother loved her poultry rearing. I was never very keen, especially after being knocked down a few times by a big stag (male) turkey who used to lie in wait for me no matter which gate or door I used. I think he had a shorter life than usual!

In the 1940s all our turkeys were black or very dark grey, known as bronze. Quicker maturing, anaemic-looking white breeds came later. Guinea fowl, the noisy, but useful, early warners of intruders, bred freely at Hacknell. They were experts at hiding their eggs in hedges fields away from the farm until, laying a clutch of approximately fifteen, they then would go broody and hatch them before proudly clucking their offspring to the farm yard for food.

Runner ducks had to be kept shut in until they had laid their eggs, usually by 11 a.m. (if my memory is correct). They travelled long distances shovelling for slugs and snails in the muckiest of places and were always the last of the poultry to return home to roost.

Poultry picking usually lasted at least two days: one for "rough" picked – head and feet left on and entrails left in – for the dealer or butcher, and another day for those birds which were ordered and had to be clean plucked and dressed off.

Tables, slabs and shelves were cleared in the dairy, the coldest room, a large joint of meat had been cooked the day before and potatoes skinned for boiling in the morning. Together with home-made chutneys and apple pie and cream, a quick and easy to serve meal was provided for at least ten to twelve people. Although no expert plucker, each December Kate Huxstep used a couple of her days off from cooking at Northcote to help. She loved the good humoured banter, the company, and an excuse to be in a real mess with feathers up to her knees.

All available helpers were roped in to help with the picking. My mother and Granny Eastman did the drawing and trussing, a skilled job made obvious by how clean and wholesome the birds looked afterwards. Even at this late stage there were problems trying to match the sizes of birds to the weight range ordered. Some customers were very fussy as to the size, others thankfully were not.

The weather was another uncertain element; a mild, mucky spell was a real worry once the poultry was dressed off. Local orders were delivered as soon as possible: some were sent by post – one could in those days! – some, sent by rail, were packed in a large wicker hamper for Granny's sister, Aunt Florrie, and her friends in London. Other orders were through Granny's stall in the market.

We always had a goose for Christmas Day, in those days goose was the cheap option, with turkey being double the price per pound.

Fifty years on I am not sure of the numbers of birds dealt with but a total of approximately one hundred seems to stick in my memory; easier to remember is the quantity of feathers in the house at Hacknell. Something I could never understand was why the picking took place in the back kitchen and not an outside shed or the barn. With the pickers having their meals around the long farmhouse table in the front kitchen, every movement swept more feathers further into the house and up the stairs.

My task, if not at school, was to prepare the giblets by pouring boiling water over the heads and feet of the ducks and geese before skinning and plucking the very short feathers covering the head and neck. The hard-bitten nails I had in those days gave me no help and fingers soon became sore. A very painful whitlow developed one year. School was far more appealing!

At Week, the picking took place in the wash-house set off from the back door, feathers still managed to get into the house but not in the quantities that there were at Hacknell.

The opening balance sheet of 1946/47 accounts shows poultry valued at £68 and sheep at £76. Income for the year – £89 14s 3½d from poultry must have been a great help to pay wages and groceries.

Mum carried on rearing poultry for several years. For her, as for many other farmers' wives, it was a little money they could call their own. Certainly it was very hard-earned money and I was not sorry when we ceased having feathers for Christmas decorations.

In the new year we had an annual visit from a mother and daughter from Exeter who bought feathers – in bags. Duck and goose without wing feathers were the most profitable, but even wing feathers were, I believe, sold for dart flights. They had a large car into which they packed bags tight to the roof and even on the passenger seat, with daughter perched on top.

PORTSMOUTH ARMS

Portsmouth Arms station on the southern line in the Taw valley, named after Lord Portsmouth, Lord of the Manor and chief landowner in Burrington, opened on 1st August 1854, was a very familiar destination from Hacknell and continued so for several years after we came to Week.

Portsmouth Arms Station

The station was a far different place in 1946 with several attractive stone built buildings; sadly all demolished some years ago. The approach from the road and car parking area was through a door in the centre of a single-storey building stretching the whole width of this parking area. The door opened into a square entrance hall with a large set of platform weights on the right-hand side against the wall of the ticket and booking office. Another door and arched hatchway opened into this office. To the left of the entrance door, above a long painted wooden form, were advertisements and a railway timetable pasted to the notice-board; at eye level if you were an adult! Another door led into the waiting room, complete with a fireplace – unused in those days, and furnished with a central square table and a few plain chairs. Diagonally across this room was another door into the Ladies' toilet. Oil lamps lit these rooms and the platforms in wintertime.

From the entrance hall, wide sliding doors with a glazed top half opened onto the platform. A penny-in-the-slot machine for Cadbury's cream chocolate had stood here before sweet rationing came into force.

To the left, past the Gentlemens' toilet with its raised glass roof at the end of the long stone range, was the wooden-clad signal box. A good fire burned in the grate of the signalman's domain in winter, and the handles of the row of levers shone bright with constant polishing. I remember a yellow duster always being used to grip the levers – at least by Mr. Fred Southcombe. Situated at the end of the "down" platform and reached by a flight of steps, a clear view of the line and signals could be had from the three windowed sides of the box.

Turning right from the entrance hall, past the station house where Mr. Southcombe lived, the railway line had to be crossed to reach the opposite "up" platform. Here were more stone buildings; firstly a goods shed, then an open-fronted passenger waiting shelter with a solid form as seating.

A laurel hedge grew the whole length of this platform, with well-filled flowerbeds on both platforms. Prizes were awarded annually by the Railway Company for the best-kept stations. Mr. Southcombe won an award several times.

A full time porter was employed as well as a signalman, to deal with goods and passengers arriving and departing. I believe that farmers in the Taw Valley sent their milk churns to the Ambrosia Dairy at Lapford by train; feeding stuffs, artificial manure and many other goods arrived at Portsmouth Arms. During the winter we sent hampers with dozens of rabbits to a firm in Cambridge – and at Christmas, poultry was sent to London. I am not sure if we sent flatpols by rail, but I know Dudley Hellyer sent many thousands by train.

From Hacknell we walked to the station by way of Bewdown and Northcote Woods – fine going down but a long climb home. By horse and cart we used Lockbar lane, coming out just above the Sawmills office – Boutchland side.

The last train of the evening was known as the "mail" train, collecting letters cleared from the postbox in the wall of the station at 8.30 p.m. People came from miles around to use this much later posting time.

After we came to Week, I used the station weekly during termtime, catching the 7.50 a.m. to Crediton on Monday mornings – by the skin of my teeth usually. Sometimes Dad had to race to South Molton Road in his Morris Minor, where the train would have been slightly delayed by a phone call from Portsmouth Arms! The train departure time was in the middle of morning milking – by hand in those days!

The return on Friday evenings was much more leisurely. I could wait at the station to be fetched if it was dark, or if light, walk home, sometimes having the company of Archie Tapscott, a driver for W. Parker, who like me had to walk up the long hill from Kingford to Week Park Cross.

When the monthly market was held in the quarry where the Sawmill is now, cattle and sheep were trucked away from Portsmouth Arms. Although the market had ceased in 1935(?), the loading pens were still there beyond the station house, as was a crane for loading and unloading heavy items. All these, along with the nostalgic steam engined trains of those days, are just distant memories of half a century ago.

John Chapple of Boutchland remembers droving cattle from Dodscott Farm, St.Giles before the goods yard closed in 1961. We were still droving sheep and cattle to South Molton Road Market and Umberleigh Market for some while after coming to Week, the few vehicles that were met waited patiently to be waved on at a convenient place, or for the animals to pass them in the opposite direction. How times have changed!

CLOTHING BOOK
1946-47
GENERAL CB 1 9

...ot until the holder's name, full
...ion Number have been
...en it safely. It

This b...
postal...
written...
is you...

HOL...

A...

R.B.1
16

MINISTRY OF
FOOD
1953 - 1954

SERIAL NO.   1

AV 092873

RATION BOOK

Surnam...

Address...

....

IF FO...
RETUR...
ANY...
OFFI...

NATIONAL
REGISTRATION

IDENTITY
CARD

WAR TIME

The recent evacuation of Instow (September '99), because of the discovery of a World War II landmine on the foreshore, revives memories of North Devon beaches being laid with anti-tank mines and cordoned off with barbed wire. Any access for the public was forbidden by illustrated signs, erected to warn of the dangers of land-mines.

At Braunton, visiting my mother's parents and sisters, I heard stories of dogs running onto nearby beaches being blown to pieces, maybe exaggerated, but I am sure with *some* truth. Some beaches were cleared, if only partially, after the dangers of invasion passed, but I am not sure when. Outings by train to Instow and Ilfracombe were enjoyed just before or just after we came to Week.

My first memory of seeing the sea was possibly in 1942 when Granny Eastman went to visit the tenants of her late brother's house on the edge of the Teign estuary at Bishopsteignton, a delightfully-named smallholding; Happy Valley. Having excitedly packed a small cardboard suitcase with a nightie and change of clothes, I also packed a silky gold elastic, ruched swimsuit (passed on from a teenaged Aunt) which I had never had the opportunity to wear in water. I thought it was to keep me dry and was very surprised that it did not!

From Portsmouth Arms we travelled to Exeter Central station, where the long flight of steps must have been an effort for Granny carrying a heavy suitcase packed, not only with her clothes, but also with two dozen or so Hacknell-produced eggs as a gift for our hosts. These were a welcome addition to their diet as shelled eggs were rationed from 1941 – I think one per person, per week.

We were immediately aware of the bombing devastation of Exeter as we walked to the bus depot in Paul Street, and even more so when sat in the stationary bus for a considerable time waiting for the rubble to be cleared in the High Street. Time enough for us to share a small thermos of "Camp" coffee.

It was at this stage that Granny discovered an earlier hefty bump had broken some of the eggs, wrapped in newspaper and packed inside her clothes. You can imagine the sticky mess by the time we had travelled to the bus stop nearest Happy Valley and then walked the final part.

I can still picture her, with the suitcase on the table, scooping out the gooey muck into a bowl for the dog – luckily not all were smashed. No such thing as cardboard ½ doz. egg boxes then nor 2½ doz. Keyes trays. Boxes were sturdily made of wood with inner divisions of slotted card, not something easily hidden, for I believe it was illegal for registered producers even to give eggs away during rationing. No doubt a few of these eggs, plus some home cooking, were intended for "Captain" Bennett, a long-time friend of Granny's late brother, Alfred Way. I can remember visiting him in a black painted shack on the very edge of the Teign estuary. He was in bed and very ill when we saw him. I had a paddle in the shallow water while they talked – but where Granny could keep an eye on me!

Happy Valley lived up to its name, in a sunny sheltered spot, where a clear wide stream ran through the outer yard and "old man's beard" flourished in the trees beyond – my first sight of this wild clematis. Having been told beforehand – probably by "the boys" at Hacknell – that the water was supplied to the house by a "ram" which lived in the house where the stream emerged from the hillside, I was very disappointed to discover that it was a submerged water-powered pump, not a sheep on a treadmill!

And at Burrington I recall lorries and jeeps full of American soldiers parked by the village hall, handing out gum to us children, the first that most of us had ever chewed. We were told they were "on manoeuvres", a new word for us, and not sure what it meant – to my young aunts at Braunton it probably had an entirely different meaning!

Anderson shelters were stacked against the outside of the hall for some time but I have no recollection of any air raid drill where they were put to use. Maybe older parishioners will remember.

Gas mask drill took place several times. I was very envious of evacuee children, some of whom had "Mickey Mouse" type masks.

At some time, probably 1942/43, a large draw took place for the war effort. The draw took place in the Square. Col. Gracey sat at a table with other helpers – it was luckily a sunny day. I had been sent up to the village, just in case we were fortunate in the draw.

There were many prizes but none came back to Hacknell. I only remember one prize, sent or brought back to his family by a local soldier; it was a banana, dark brown and withered. Several years later I discovered bananas were yellow before they became brown. An unexpected sighting one day was a barrage balloon, broken free from its moorings somewhere miles away. It drifted slowly over the playground trailing a long rope below.

My young aunts,
Edith and Evelyn

My father, Abie and John were in the Home Guard along with many other Burrington men. They had to attend lectures, training and drill in the evenings and occasionally be on duty all night. A small hut was transported to the waste ground at Red Post as a shelter for them. On clear nights the glow in the sky from the bombed cities of Plymouth in the south and Cardiff in the north could be seen from Red Post. Abie having a motorbike was a dispatch rider or messenger.

Searchlights from the battery at Ley could be seen raking the sky in search of enemy planes on many nights. Blackout restrictions were strenuously enforced. Tightly woven black material was either made into curtains or stretched on a frame to fit exactly over windows at night to exclude every chink of light.

Householders were encouraged to criss-cross sticky tape over the glass in their windows to prevent injury from shattered glass in the event of an explosion. At Hacknell it was decided to take the risk, but some houses in the village taped theirs. Mrs. Harris at Ticavin cottages was one I remember having it done.

TRAVELLING

Never having travelled further than Torrington, Ilfracombe, Exeter and Bishopsteignton before 1946, the prospect of a week's holiday in London before changing schools and being bridesmaid to Beattie and John, filled me with great excitement.

During that August, Granny's sister and her husband had been staying at Hacknell on holiday – which they often did – but for some reason needed to return to London for a week – a welcome respite for all at Hacknell!

We set off early one morning, Uncle Billy driving his pre-war dark green Wolseley car with real walnut veneered dashboard. It had a small rear window, obscured inside when necessary by a rise and fall cloth blind, operated on a cord and pulley system by the driver from his seat.

Because of petrol rationing and the risk of being destroyed in the blitz, this car had been laid up during the war in the garage at Hacknell. John used to start it at intervals and kept the car in such good running order it was eventually driven back to London without any problems on the way, he told me.

Aunt Florrie, as always, occupied the front passenger seat, armed with a tin of sweets to be unwrapped at intervals and popped into Uncle Billy's mouth – and mine occasionally, when I refused to be distracted!

On a long journey she passed the time with a slow, careful manicure, pushing back the cuticles and going around each nail in turn with a file, then an emery board, finishing off with a chamois leather buffer. This fancy nonsense was something no other lady did, in my experience!

We travelled by way of Exeter, Honiton and Windwhistle, where we pulled into a gateway to have a snack (packed at Hacknell) and I was instructed to admire the view. Uncle Billy probably did the same, the other side of the car.

I saw my very first combine harvester working on Salisbury Plain – another ten years before they became commonplace in Burrington – and I remember the mile after mile of straight roads up and down, hill after gentle hill. I was amazed; Morchard Road was the longest stretch of unbending road I knew before then.

Stopping at Stonehenge, we were able to walk amongst the stones without, as far as I remember, any hindrance or payment.

I was taken to the Zoo, Madam Tussaud's (but not the Chamber of Horrors – I might have had nightmares!), the Tower of London and Tower Bridge. I walked up the Mall to Buckingham Palace, had tea at Lyons' Corner House where an orchestra was playing, travelled by double-decker bus and on the underground – all completely new experiences for me. The car was only used for the journeys to and from Devon to conserve petrol coupons.

I remember the huge areas of bomb sites all over the city, but not so much in the residential area of North London where they lived. Much has been forgotten of that holiday, I wish that notes had been made or a diary kept, but one thing I vividly remember is being made to sit in the upstairs toilet until a successful result had been achieved!

Aunty and Uncle were childless and, as is often the case, considered themselves experts at child rearing. Never having had anyone the least bit interested in the state of my bowels during the previous eleven years, when questioned on the first morning, I honestly replied "No". So I was ordered to sit there, supplied with copies of "Homes and Gardens", and "The Lady". Even for such an avid reader as I was by then, "The Lady" did not inspire me at all in any way.

I soon learnt that well rustled stiff Harpic toilet paper and a firm pull on the chain, early in the morning, satisfied my Great Aunt and I was able to obey my own body clock later at my leisure!

The next summer, 1947, Nan and Charlie Wellington invited me to Cheltenham, travelling back with them after visiting his parents at Colleton Mills toll house. Their visits to us continued as long as Charlie was able to drive to Devon.

It was another two or three years before I ventured out of Devon again, this time to Cornwall on an outing arranged by Mrs.Webber at the Barnstaple Inn. I was fascinated by the bright blue waters of the china clay pits and the almost lunar landscape of the pure white conical spoil heaps around St.Austell.

Exmoor was another discovery, about the same time, on a coach outing from Ilfracombe with Granny Eastman – we were staying with an aunt at Braunton for a few days. After petrol was de-rationed in 1950, we were able to "gad" about more, even to South Molton!

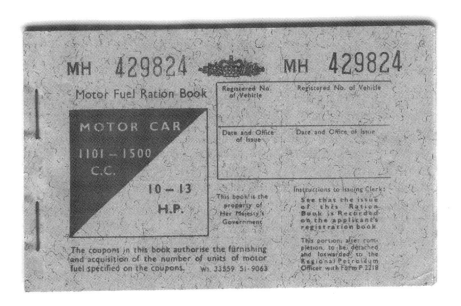

Grandfather Hewitt in uniform before going to France in 1915.
Children left to right are Doris, Cissy and Rose

IN SICKNESS AND IN HEALTH

We came to Week two years before the National Health Service began in 1948. With its concept of free health, optical and dental care from "the cradle to the grave", this must have been a great relief for the majority of North Devon residents – as for the rest of the country – despite the compulsory weekly contribution by all those in employment.

My grandfather (Hewitt), a staunch Liberal, insisted on giving his first child Lloyd, as one of her Christian names, in honour of Prime Minister Lloyd George who introduced the 1911 National Insurance Act. So my mother was registered as ROSE MARY LLOYD HEWITT. Being severely wounded in one leg in World War I and disabled for the rest of his life, what a difference free health care would have made to Granny and their eight children.

My mother paid regularly into the Nursing Association funds for a district nurse and Hospital Aid for in-patient care, but I was never aware of bills being presented by Dr. R. Graham-Pole or his successor, Dr. Morris. They certainly had to be paid somehow for visits to Hacknell, and later to Week, and for treatment given. Maybe there was another scheme to cover care by a Doctor.

Over the years, our family had their share of illness. Bernie had broken his leg soon after coming to Hacknell in 1932. Granny spent some time at Exeter Eye Infirmary after an accident chopping sticks in the back kitchen. I remember seeing her sitting on the chopping block with blood oozing through her fingers and running down her cheek, waiting to be taken to the Doctor and from there to hospital where she had to have her eye removed. After some time a very natural looking artificial eye was fitted. She also had a huge goitre on her neck – common-place in those days, but rarely seen now – as well as a very deformed ankle from a badly set broken bone, the result of her horse bolting, throwing her from the trap when returning to Shuteley Farm from Torrington Market.

My Uncle Abie had alopecia when a late teenager, losing all his hair. He had a course of "Violet Ray" treatment some time later. I remember the excitement when a little downy fluff began to grow, but the excitement was short-lived when this too fell out, never to grow again. I remember how acutely embarrassed he was at his baldness. If we had visitors he kept his cap on all the time, indoors as well as out. We took no notice, he was just Abie – without hair.

My father had treatment for ulcers – he had to drink lots of milk, which now, I believe, is regarded as one of the worst things to drink for this painful complaint, apart from alcohol!

Mum had her appendix removed in the North Devon Infirmary in 1939 or 40, followed by phlebitis, for which the treatment in those days was to stay in bed with sandbags to keep the leg still (which I thought excessive fuss for a flea bite) – far different from today's advice. She was very ill with pneumonia shortly before we moved to Week.

Despite being only 2lb. when I was born, in January, in a big draughty farmhouse, I was a healthy child. The only time I remember being at the surgery for treatment while at Hacknell, was to have stitches in my forehead after being knocked unconscious by falling backwards from the tallet against the stone wall down into the feeding path for the shippon below.

Doctors seemed to be much more accessible to their patients pre-N.H.S., and for many years afterwards, with morning and evening surgery on most weekdays as far as I remember. No appointments were necessary, surgery began at a stated time and went on till everyone had been seen (evening surgery still going on at 9.00 p.m. was not unusual at Dr. Wingfield's at Chulmleigh) and sent away with their prescription made up by the same doctor. Medicine was in a bottle marked in spoonfuls, tightly corked, wrapped in white paper, sealed with sealing wax. Pills were counted into round card boxes.

John dousing us with confetti, ready to go on honeymoon.
Granny Eastman with black handbag, her goitre and turned ankle very evident.

It was said that doctors always asked for a urine specimen to be brought on future visits as a means of getting bottles returned!

In 1948 our family became patients of Dr. Wingfield at Chulmleigh after being unhappy with the lack of care my father received when suffering from Quinsy, an abscess in the throat, and the death of my grandfather, aged 63, from peritonitis, having been treated for a non-existent ulcer all the preceding week.

In the 1940s and 50s polio was a dreaded disease – even more so than meningitis today. The cause was uncertain and treatment, before vaccines and penicillin were discovered, ineffective. Those who survived were kept alive by being encased in an iron lung, a machine the size of a large single bed in which the patient lay day and night for months on end.

TB was still prevalent, with patients being sent to Sanatoriums at Hawley, Barnstaple and Hawkmoor on Dartmoor to recuperate with complete bed rest and pure air.

Measles, whooping cough, diphtheria, scarletina, mumps and chicken pox were all nasty, unpreventable childhood illnesses.

Boils, carbuncles and whitlows were frequent before antibiotics, often needing to be lanced. Men suffered particularly from carbuncles on the back of the neck where stiff collars rubbed germs into the skin. Few country children escaped the winter affliction of chilblains and seasonal infections of ringworm. At one time Bernie had a huge septic ringworm on his head while I had them around my neck. The memory of the pain caused by the green copper-based lotion used to treat them is with me still. Nowadays, counselling for stress and trauma would surely be offered!

AROUND THE PARISH

In 1946 many houses in the village and parish were thatched. Mains electric, water and sewage systems had not arrived but Mr.Jim Western supplied some village properties with electricity generated by an engine housed in a shed behind his petrol pump, opposite the oak tree.

Burrington Square with petrol pumps and generator house, behind the ancient tree.

He and his family ran the post office, where stationery, sweets and drapery were also for sale. Mr. Western was a cobbler by trade, making and repairing all kinds of boots and shoes in his workshop at the back of the house.

At Church Gate cottage lived Jack Cooke and his wife, Rose. Jack was a tailor, making suits, sports jackets, trousers and breeches for many local men. He stocked a special thorn-proof tight-woven worsted to make jackets for gamekeepers in a dull dark green. My father had a jacket made for himself which wore for years needing only a stiff brushing to be kept clean.

As well as making new clothes, Mr. Cooke repaired garments; corduroy working breeches were re-fronted by replacing the section above the buttoned fitted leg part to wherever necessary up to the waistband and seamed in at each side. I believe Mrs. John Watkins still has a pair of new unworn breeches, with the original bill from Mr. Cooke.

Copperfields was at that time a grocers and ironmongers run by Mr. Gilbert Parker and his family from the room on the right hand side of the door. The Barnstaple Inn, a Starkey, Knight & Ford pub, much smaller then with all the north end being sheds and storerooms, was run by Mr. & Mrs. Jim Webber with their family of unusually named children: Mowbray John, Hilton Morland, Sidonia Melva Gwen, Norma Pam Joy, Anita Cherry Reese, Patricia Judith Dawn and Karen Nancy (Queenie).

The smooth piece of cement on the end of the shed behind the signpost facing Pound Lane, was used by Hannaford, Ward & Southcombe to stick posters advertising markets and farm sales. No doubt the auctioneers paid rent for this privilege as they did to Col. Gracey for a board in the former market at Portsmouth Arms – now the Sawmills. The shed was used by Palfreyman & Joint as a store, as was the "Old Reading room" – now London House Cottage. In Mr. Tancock's field beside this stone shed was a Nissan hut which was used to store ammunition, entered through a small gate in the hedge.

Mr .& Mrs. Miller ran the London House Stores – grandparents of Anne and Denise – stocking just about everything that country people needed. I believe Mrs. Miller was a soft touch for late night shoppers at her side door, probably some who could just as easily have come earlier in the day. Next door, Mr.Fred Harris ran his coal business, coal having to be fetched from the goods yard at the station. In those days of petrol rationing I remember him delivering by horse and butt. The butt being kept in a shed between the back of Ticavin Cottages and the tarmac part of the playground; a shed us children sneaked into when Mrs. Lizzy Friend or Miss Gillies were not watching – which was not often!

A resident policeman, Frank Holman, lived in the village, and district nurse, Ada Carter, lived at No.1. Balls Corner.

William Parker's Transport was based in the quarry at Bridge, the small wooden office is still there as is the Church of England Mission Church on the opposite side of the road. Built in the 1860s and finally closed in the 1960s, it was still being used for monthly services in 1946. The ornate altar and reredos were removed to the parish church after the closure, and Mr. John Watkins managed to buy the bell, after the vicar had sold it to a dealer.

The station at Portsmouth Arms was quite busy then with passengers and goods, and has been dealt with more fully in another article. The pub there was very plain and simple, geared to the local working man – as many rural pubs were. Being part of the Northcote estate, Col. Gracey held twice-yearly Lady Day and Michaelmas dinners there when tenants paid their rents. Northcote Manor was a private house until Col. Gracey's death in 1962.

Week Cross was so narrow before being widened twice – in 1967 and 1970 – visibility improved more when the Murch's thatched cottage was demolished in 1981. The first bulldozers were being used in the mid forties; Col. Gracey hired one, with operator, from Roach's at Wellpark, Crediton in 1947/48 to level several hedges on his farms – some fields were only one or two acres, almost impossible to work even with small tractors.

There was no passing lay-by between the two lanes to Week. Larger vehicles were unable to pass in the narrower section even though it had been a part of the Exeter to Barnstaple Stagecoach route branching to Torrington from Week Cross. The granite milestones purchased by the Turnpike Trust are all still in position in the parish at Dole park cross, opposite the stone depot above Bryher Cottage, set into the London House shop wall (a former Inn) and at the top of Bircham Hill. The next is this side of the river Taw at Handsford in Ashreigney parish.

Back in the village, the temporary corrugated asbestos village hall had been erected after the earlier building burnt to the ground in

Week Cross before the road was widened

Week Cross afterwards – before the house was knocked down.

Week Cross now

November 1944. On the Green, there was no play equipment and the rough grass was cut only once a year for Burrington Fair.

The school was just the main building – no kitchen or extra classroom then – and having seven children going to secondary education that year from a total of less than thirty, the space was probably adequate.

The Vicarage – now Meadow House – was then occupied by the resident Vicar for Burrington, Rev. Wrenford, and had been a larger house at one time, being one or two rooms longer to the east. I remember Sylvia Heal using long-handled pruners to prune a shrub which grew against the front of the house. I had been sent by Miss Gilles with a message for the Vicar. Many years later as correspondent to the School Governors, I was able to read in the "Minutes of governors' meetings" for that time, many notes of complaint by both the Vicar and Miss Gilles regarding their conduct to each other. This obviously made interesting reading for me, and explained the coolness and studied politeness between those two when the Vicar made his frequent visits to the school.

Around the parish some families remain at the same address, even if the second or third generation. Baileys delivered milk from Crosspark, Crockers were at Northcote Farm, Elworthys at Upcott, Harrises and Friends at Ticavin Cottages, Millers at the shop, Snells at Elscott, Shorts at Homelands, Hillcrest and Catham, Tancocks at the Barton (Marilyn Smale, née Tancock) and at Lakepark, Thomases at Pavington, Webbers at Curzeland, Pincombes at Abbotsmarsh and, of course, Eastmans (Bolt) at Week Farm.

Snells at Elscott are the winners by a wide margin, having been there since the 1840s – the rest of us are newcomers!

Some businesses have disappeared, some buildings have changed usage. Others have been built: the Radar Station on Burrington Moor, Eaglescott Airfield, Aylescott Driers, the industrial units at the bottom of Bircham Hill, the galvanized sheds at Pickards, Portsmouth Arms Sawmills, Acorn Woodcraft, Riverside Garage (now closed) and the sewage works building at Town Bridge are just some of the changes since we came to Week.

Postman Gordon Webber delivering mail to the
Civil Aviation Authority Radar Station on Burrington Moor

THRESHING AND REED COMBING

Threshing days provided a kind of benchmark against which all other busy days were measured, by both the men outdoors and the women indoors.

They were usually one day at a time, maybe three or four times a year, depending on the amount of cereals grown, having possibly had a week's notice from the threshing contractor that, weather permitting, the thresher would be at your farm on a certain day, following on from other farms in the neighbourhood.

Before the war, farmers were able to choose their contractor, but to avoid wasting coal for the steam engine, or fuel for the subsequent Marshall tractor, by overlapping areas, the War Agricultural Committee allocated compact areas of farms to threshing tackle operators; so, previously having employed Leonard Murch of Umberleigh, Hacknell became part of Harold Stenner's area. For myself it made little difference who did the threshing, but if the arrival coincided with "home from school" time the driver of the traction engine made a great difference. Maurice Thorne, Stenners' driver, would let me ride on the footplate and even to steer the gleaming, steam monster down Hacknell's long lane. I remember the steering wheel had a small handle protruding from it to help swing the wheel round and round to make even the slightest adjustment to direction.

For the farmer there were many days of preparation beforehand; arrangements with other farmers for helpers on the day were made. Those workers probably had several consecutive days of threshing while the machine was in the area. Steam coal had to be bought, bags checked for holes and mended if necessary, or sacks hired from a merchant if grain was to be sold. These sacks held 4 bushels: $2^1/_2$ cwt. of wheat, 2 cwt. (100 kgs.) of barley and $1^1/_2$ cwt. of oats. No health and safety rules in those days regarding the weight one person should carry!

Water for the boiler of the engine was another essential requirement; at Hacknell this meant clearing all the odds and ends dumped outside the tool house at the end of the enclosed back yard behind the house. This was to enable the hidden wooden door closing the well head to be opened. This was the only time and purpose I can remember the well being used; for some reason it was not used for the house.

A large reinforced hose was attached to the engine, the other end dropped into the well to draw up water – almost like an elephant drinking through its trunk! At Week, the well by the road was easily accessible.

Another essential need was close mesh wire netting to surround the base of the rick being threshed, to prevent rats escaping. This was a legal requirement to conserve this country's limited and precious food supplies, enforced by the local policeman who could – and did – make unannounced spot checks when threshing was in progress. Farm dogs and terriers would have a field day killing them. Rats were a great problem without the control of modern warferin products. This law continued some years after the war ended for I remember the police coming to Week. An added incentive to kill rats was the payment of one penny per tail by the Ministry. I think us children shared this bounty.

Other farm work had to be organized and as much as possible done beforehand, leaving only feeding, milking and cleaning out the shippons on threshing days.

For Mum and Granny, days of cooking and skinning buckets of potatoes preceded the arrival of the thresher or reed comber, with anything up to sixteen men to feed for three meals. The engine driver and his mate came early to get steam up; if they were able to fix the engine and thresher between the Dutch Barns at Hacknell or ricks at Week on the day before, these men would have a fried breakfast about 7.00 a.m.

Lunch for everyone at 10.00 – 10.30 a.m. was taken out in large, square, cloth-lined baskets containing huge pasties, cut into generous portions, cheese, meat, egg and jam sandwiches, slices of fruit cake and small cakes, sliced and buttered yeast buns and scones, all washed down with ad lib mugs of tea from enamel cans or a heavy earthenware pitcher. All the men had hearty country appetites, stimulated by the hard, continuous work. As part of the team of workers, there was no chance to slack at all; every man's job needed to keep pace with the rest

Dinner had to be ready promptly at 1.00 p.m. when, having washed the dust from their eyes, the men trooped in to sit around the kitchen table. This meal would have been a roast in winter or cold meat with boiled potatoes, chutney and beetroot in warmer weather, followed by rice pudding and apple dumplings, or apple tart, custard and cream.

Sometime in the afternoon, tea was taken out to the men, depending on the time of year, for without the benefit of electric light, threshing was unable to continue as late in the short days of mid-winter. This meal was a repeat of the 10.00 a.m. meal, again everything home made, except the bread for sandwiches and this before the invention of sliced bread!

What with washing all those dishes, feeding calves and poultry, etc., what a long, tiring day it must have been for Mum and Granny and an even greater disaster if rain was so heavy the rick could not be threshed; all that cooking to be prepared again if the delay was more than a couple of days. No fridge or freezer then to store food. Even so, nothing would have been wasted with so many in our household to be fed every day at Hacknell.

Other farmers' wives may have catered differently. I have heard of one farm where each man's food was wrapped individually and a very small package at that – but not in Burrington I hasten to add!

The busy time did not finish with the thresher leaving the mowstead (rickyard). The straw rick had to be thatched or the wads of straw loaded on carts and taken to various tallets. If grain or straw had been borrowed from a neighbour, this would be returned and the remaining corn in bags carried up the granary steps to be tipped through the trap door into corn hutches below.

The threshing area with many moving belts and spinning pulleys was too dangerous for children to be running around, so one of my tasks – if not at school – was to refill cider jars, when the thirsty workers had emptied them, from barrels in the cellar. Most men who threshed for us drank cider; the alternative would have been cold tea or scalded milk. I believe it was the custom to give the workers extra money for what was usually a dusty, dirty, hard day's work.

I cannot begin to remember the names of all the men involved and the tasks they performed, but as an example of men needed for threshing and reed combing, I am indebted to a local farmer, Dudley Hellyer of Twitchen farm, Burrington, who kept a diary for most of his life.

His entry for December 30th, 1946 reads:-

"Threshing – Harold Stenner and G. Pike feeding, J. Parkhouse cutting binds. C. Skinner, E. Tucker and S. Bailey pitching, S. Bawden, P.O.W. (Prisoner of War), P. Vicary, W. Patt and W. Govier straw, self and W. Chapple corn, father doing bullocks"

and for September 22nd 1943:-

"Reed combing, Wallace and self at sacks, Stan Bawden and Alf Webber pitching, H. Parkhouse cutting binds, P. Parkhouse, S. Bailey, J. Parkhouse and W. Rice tying reed, Charlie Webber paring reed, J. Baker making reed rick, * Hunkins [He worked for John Watkins and lived at Northparks] making straw rick, Brian Bailey, Douglas Bailey, Norman Watkins and Mrs. Bawden at straw, father stripping ricks, etc".

He did not mention anyone keeping the douse clear (DOUSE was the waste corn husks and weed seeds). This was usually a boy's job, probably one of those mentioned as 'at straw'.

GARDENS AND GARDENERS

Although by 1946 the "Dig for Victory" campaign urging people to grow as much food as possible to feed a nation at war had eased, most country people had a vegetable garden, supplying much of their needs, indeed the majority took great pride in doing so. Farm workers sometimes would accept or refuse employment – with a tied cottage – according to the size of the garden, the number of drills of potatoes allowed to be tilled (planted) in the root field and availability of a hedge to be cut and laid in their spare time during the winter for the next year's firewood. All these helped with their finances, especially if they had a family to support.

Kingsland, where Ern and Liz Miller already lived before the Eastmans came to Hacknell, had been a smallholding at one time but became a worker's cottage when the land was transferred to Hacknell. With two large gardens, a good sized orchard, pig and poultry houses, a three-bedroomed house in a warm, south facing, sunny spot, Kingsland was in a league of its own for a tied cottage; the only drawback was its isolated position accessible only by way of a rough cart track from either the Red Post to Forches Road, or from Hacknell lane. Ern and Liz lived there happily for many years until his retirement when they moved first to Pennyhop and then New Buildings.

Flower gardening was of secondary importance to most and usually behind the safety of a fence or wall in those days for, with the daily passage through the village of working horses, herds of milking cows and flocks of sheep, today's hanging baskets and flower tubs by the roadside and open plan gardens wouldn't stand a chance of flourishing – like some farmers' gardens I know!

Dad and his brothers were keen gardeners, no doubt inherited from their grandfather Eastman, who kept a market garden, orchards and fruit tree nursery at Smallmarsh, High Bickington. They grew all kinds of fruit and vegetables, keeping our large family supplied all year round, the surplus being sold on Granny's stall in Barnstaple market.

Eastman great-grandparents
who lived at Smallmarsh, High Bickington

Raspberries, strawberries, blackcurrants and gooseberries were sold in llb. chip punnets and larger chip baskets of thin white woven wood, often lined with leaves of whichever fruit they contained. Damsons, plums, pears, apples, blackberries and mushrooms were all used to vary our diet and to be sold on the stall. A wonderfully flavoured Golden Gage plum grew in the orchard with fruit the size of peaches.

A special treat, which we all looked forward to Granny bringing home from the market at the end of July, were mazzards, a local black cherry, which would be gently cooked and eaten with clotted cream, or made into tarts or pies. A taste so delicious it cannot be described adequately, but remains a mouth drooling memory even after so many years.

Elderberries were gathered to make wine in autumn, used more for medicinal purposes than as a social drink. The only other wine I can recall Granny making was white grape wine, using sour green grapes which grew at Rags Cottage on Shortridge Hill, Umberleigh, where she was born. Her brother, Albert, was the last of the Way family to live in the cottage. This particular year there was a bumper crop; hampers full of them were brought to Hacknell, far too many probably! I know there was a desperate search for containers to ferment the grapes, but I have no idea if the wine was fit to drink or not. The vine is still growing in the same place today.

Old roses bloomed on the plum garden hedge at Hacknell, no doubt relegated from the flower garden at some time. One, a large single bright pink, another a paler pink with vermillion stripe and, at Week, again on the garden hedge, a fully double, beautifully scented pink rose is still giving pleasure fifty years later. These roses I believe to be very old varieties, having seen illustrations like them in specialist rose books.

A peculiar primrose grew at Hacknell against the edge of the lawn. It had a ring of tiny leaves framing the flower. Now I know it to be the very old variety Jack in the Green, well known in Shakespeare's day but obviously not at Hacknell in the twentieth century.

Cattle in the yard in happier times

MILK MARKETING BOARD   10/ 9504

Regional Officer
Mr. W. CHANNON.
Prudential Buildings,
Bedford Street,
Plymouth.
Telephone: Plymouth 2158/9

Head Office :
THAMES DITTON, SURREY.
Telephone : EMBERBROOK 4181.

CONFIRMATION.

_____ 194_

DIRECTION OF MILK SUPPLY MAY 1946
(PRODUCER'S COPY)

PERSON(S)
TO WHOM
MILK MUST
BE SUPPLIED

Name   The Torridge Vale Dairies,   No. 650110
Address   Torrington,   Ltd.,
                Devon.

Premises at

        Torrington.   3A

You are hereby directed to supply milk produced at Week Farm.
_____ to the person(s) named above as and from the
27th March, 1946 until further notice.

QUANTITY.
    (a) The whole of the milk you produce for sale by wholesale.
    (b) The milk surplus to your requirements.
    (c) As defined in a supplementary Premium Contract.
    (d)_____

DELIVERY.
    (a) You are required to deliver the milk to :—
        (i) the premises named above.
        (ii) _____ Railway Station.
    (b) The milk will be collected at your farm or farm collecting point by :—
        (i) the person(s) named above.
        (ii) _____

                        MILK MARKETING BOARD,

                        _____
                        Regional Marketing Officer.

To Name   A.G. Eastman, Esq.,
Address   Week Farm,
          High Bickington,
          Umberleigh, Devon.   No. 10/71129

FRIENDS AND NEIGHBOURS

Knowing probably 95% of people in Burrington parish in 1946, and almost every child, it would be a daunting task to write even a brief memory of each one. Some I can recall vividly, others hardly at all, but all recalled with pleasure, which I hope any relatives remaining will share with me.

The lane at Hacknell was maintained by the council almost as far as the house. For some reason their responsibility ended at the bottom of Sandpark, where in the past there had been a gate, one of at least three blocking the lane; others were at each end of Hamlyns Moor – only the gate posts remained at that time.

The council roadman was Walter Miller who lived in Barton Road. He kept the water tables clear and gutters cleaned out on a regular basis, so we children would meet him when we travelled to and from school, and never passed without asking him "What's the time please, Mr. Miller?" just to see him take a watch on a chain from his waistcoat pocket, click open the case and hold it out sideways almost at arm's length, for he was very cross-eyed and this was his only way to see the watch face. We were fascinated and amused by this and lucky he didn't swipe us with his shovel, but he was never other than long-suffering and polite.

Several members of the Smith family I remember for their dry sense of humour and fun. Miss Annie Smith is mentioned elsewhere as a collector of funds for various causes. She had a way all her own of describing events humorously, an inbuilt understanding of broad Devonshire dialect was a very necessary asset to appreciate the humour.

Charlie, another member of the Smith family, lived on his own at Kingsland Cottages; his nephew Sidney joined him in later years, after we were at Week. There being little difference in distance from

Burrington to Red Post by way of Town Bridge or Forches Cross, I sometimes returned past Charlie's hoping to see his wind-powered animated figures in motion in the long narrow roadside garden. He must have spent many hours making these working models from odds and ends. One I remember in particular, was of a man and woman sharpening knives on a grindstone, he bobbing up and down offering the knife to the stone, she, turning the handle. Also in this garden was a small shed where he kept all kinds of treasures, at least I thought they were treasures. There were brightly coloured bead work purses, mats and patterned bead samplers, small native dolls and a tin of foreign coins, plus other things I have forgotten. I understood them to be First World War souvenirs. How times have changed now – these days, a middle-aged man inviting a little girl into his garden would be treated with great suspicion, not the innocent friendship it was, with not a word or action out of place.

There were numerous stories of Charlie's "luck" at having pheasants and rabbits drop dead in front of him, mostly told by him in the first instance. One was of him looking through a hole in the hedge, gun at the ready, when the police constable came up behind him, saying "I've caught you this time, Charlie. What do you see through that gap"? "You have a look, sir, I can't see nort (nothing)" He had spotted the P.C. in the distance and outfoxed him.

Charlie Heales, a gamekeeper at Northcote, lodged with Mr. & Mrs. Reg Murch at Week Cross, after being demobbed, before marrying and setting up home at Hill Sampson. Charlie was a tall, long-legged middle-aged man, who decided that the easiest way to measure the bedroom for new lino was to pace it out, a normal pace being three feet; unfortunately, his was nearer four feet, so the roll of lino arrived several feet short!

Charlie became progressively more crippled with arthritis as he became older, needing two walking sticks to get around on his feet, but surprisingly, managed to ride a bicycle for many years to give his continued loyal support to the Barnstaple Inn. From Hill Sampson to Burrington was a fairly easy cycling road as far as Town Bridge, near the village, where he dismounted with great difficulty. On the return journey he needed to walk as far as Whiteoak using his bike for support. One Sunday evening after the church harvest festival service, our family were on their way home, when they came across Charlie, knelt in the road, with his sticks laid in one direction and bike in another, having come to grief trying to remount. Five year old Norma Kingdon also in our car, viewed the scene with a puzzled expression before commenting "What a funny place for Mr.Heale to say his prayers".

Hill Sampson now

Before Charlie and Amy Heales moved into Hill Sampson, the Jewell family had lived there from approximately 1938; Arthur Jewell was a woodsman on the Northcote estate, a quietly spoken, kindly gentleman, his wife Beattie and daughters Linda and Christine lived with him, as well as Raymond Mayne, a Bristol evacuee and Mr. Herbert Bindon who had fled the blitz in London. Christine, their youngest child, maybe five or six years older than me, was an easy target for teasing by her friends. Having been for a day to Barnstaple, she remarked that Barnstaple was a mouldy place – she would rather be home in Devon!

A new experience at Week was seeing Buffy Short for the first time. A local man with relatives in the area, for some reason he chose to be "of no fixed abode" and slept in various barns around here and the Elscott area. Never having seen a tramp before, I was apprehensive at first, but he was never any trouble apart from having an effect on egg production when he was in the area. He was around for several years before dying, so I believe, in the South Molton Union.

At Lower Hacknell lived our nearest neighbours, Bill and Annie Mills. Mrs. Mills was a very smart lady, and noted for having new clothes as often as an excuse arose to do so, each outfit was completed with matching, or contrasting, hat, shoes, gloves and handbag. I was sometimes invited for tea when she had other children visiting and her house was as smart and neat as she was herself.

My mother's Uncle, John Willie Webber, thatcher and pig killer, is remembered by many local people for stories of his escapades with a motor bike and sidecar: how Fred Harris' horse towed him home, with John William steering the bike and Fred in the sidecar guiding the horse; and another time wondering who owned the wheel bowling down the hill before him, until he turned the corner at the bottom and realised it was from his sidecar! I remember him as a very kindly man, a sincere Christian, whose daily practice of kneeling by his chair for a time of silent prayer before his meal was ready; I witnessed this on several occasions when I took my packed lunch, in the days before school meals were available, to be eaten either in his cottage at Barton Road or at Ticavin Cottage with Mrs.Lizzie Friend, fondly known to all as "Granny" Friend. I think of her whenever passing a knife to anyone and remember being gently corrected when handing the knife she had requested, point first towards her. Ever since it has been handle first.

Henry Heal worked at Lower Hacknell, living in Kingsland Cottages beside Charlie Smith, with his wife Barbara and children, Sylvia and Arnold. He had a metal crate on the carrier of his bicycle to hold bottles which were filled with milk at Lower Hacknell. At Hacknell, we could hear the rattle of the empty bottles long before seeing Henry passing the yard, so punctual one could set their watch by him. He was another provider of dandelions and lettuce for my rabbits, Christopher and Mary, kept in hutches by the barn door.

Adults were always addressed as Mr., Mrs. or Miss by most children fifty years ago; some family friends were given the honorary title of Auntie and Uncle or occasionally a pet name such as mine of "Max" for Ern Miller (Max Miller – comedian) but that was about as informal as we were allowed to get.

Many people from the whole of North Devon and even further afield will remember Mr. & Mrs.Sidney Hicks, if not by name then for the sight of them on the A.377 road between Colleton and Umberleigh. He, dressed in all kinds of clothes, often sat on his bicycle holding onto the top rail of a fence, pedalling for exercise or with Mrs. Hicks, a tiny lady, pushing him.

As they grew older they walked up and down the stretch of road West of Kingford, where they lived in a caravan beside the river Taw until their deaths, Dolly on December 25th, 1976, aged 90, and Sidney on April 3rd, 1982, aged 85.

After Mrs. Hicks died – she was the driver of their small car – friends at Kingford and Portsmouth Arms saw to his welfare. Derek Ley delivered milk from his parents' farm, Michael Pearce of Cowlas taking on this task when Derek left home. Mrs.Beattie Pedlar, who was nearing 90 made a continuous supply of rice puddings and egg custard, which the boys delivered with the milk and giving him whatever help he needed. Each week Mr. Hicks prepared stencils which Michael ran off on his Gestetner machine, giving advice to customers on the most likely answers to crossword puzzles – so that they could win money prizes. Then his daughter drove over from her home near Holsworthy to prepare the sheets for posting to a large number of customers. She and her family supported as they were able, this very independent couple through the rigours of hard winters and the traumas of road accidents, almost inevitable given their disregard to the passing traffic.

Before moving to the warmer climate of the Taw Valley they had lived in a caravan by the Burrington Moor radar station, in a field still called "Hickses field" by local people. Their usual daily journey was as far as Week Cross, in our early years at Week, remembered for the problems we had droving cattle or sheep along the road to pass Mr.Hicks, lying in a gateway with his legs in the road, or being pushed on his bike, bits and pieces of clothing flapping in the wind.

Stories abound, no doubt some exaggerated, of Mr.Hicks' dislike of noise, and their use of a nearby stream to wash themselves, for I never heard anything but that they were very clean, despite their appearance. Both funerals were held at the High Bickington methodist Church conducted by Rev. Robert Thompson. Eric was a bearer for both and Dick Pidler arranged the funerals. They were buried in St. Mary's churchyard, where headstones mark the final resting place of this out of the ordinary couple.

The only photograph of me at Burrington School

MORE SCHOOL MEMORIES

I can remember a photographer coming once to school and then only taking individual photos, no groups of either class. We dressed in our outdoor clothes and sat on a chair in the playground against the cob wall. I look like a refugee child. There were regular visits by the school doctor and the "bug" nurse, Mrs. Owen. We were checked, inspected and sometimes weighed and measured, sitting in jockey style weights which were hung from a large iron staple above the door at the west end of the classroom – this staple is still there in the junior classroom, but this was the infants room at that time.

The oculist examined us at certain ages, not every year if my memory is correct, unless there was a problem, in which case we were seen at each visit; such a case was John Holland who wore glasses with one lens taped over.

The dentist spent several days at school, making it worthwhile to set up in business in the southeast corner of the junior classroom, now the dining area. The adjustable black chair facing the window, the foot-operated belt and pulley system drill apparatus behind it. Notes had been sent home via ourselves to inform parents of these inspections, with a tear-off slip to refuse or accept treatment. The majority were rather envious of those few who avoided sitting in that dreaded black chair by their parent signing the refusal slip.

On a happier note, we had a variety of comics to choose from and to swap when read. Knockout, Dandy, Beano and Hotspur with weekly fixes of Desperate Dan, Korky the cat, Keyhole Kate, etc. to entertain us. We played hopscotch, statues, kerb or wall, Mr. Wolf, Lucy Lockett, skipping and ball games in the playground during break times, releasing our energies, for in the classroom both Miss Jury and Miss Gillies kept firm control of their class. We were not expected to talk except to answer or ask questions of our teacher during lessons. So, when the giggles from a group of us grew increasingly loud, Miss Gillies became very annoyed. The cause of our giggles, an evacuee boy, Willie Sorrell, was not laughing, he was mortified, having had an unfortunate accident.

Miss Gillies strode forcefully to us, ruler at the ready, picked on one boy demanding an explanation. Supressing his mirth, he said "Please Miss, Willie 'as been and sh... sh... sh... dirt himself". I think even Miss Gillies had difficulty keeping a straight face after that.

I believe a man came from Barnstaple to collect rabbit skins and rags through the village, but at Crediton during my first year there at school, I saw other street traders. Some summer evenings the sound of a barrel organ could be heard through open windows, an elderly man wheeled the organ to the centre of The Green then turned the handle at a steady pace with one hand to produce the music, holding a collecting box in the other. A knife sharpener plied for trade around the streets using the wheel of his upturned bicycle as motivating power for the small grind stone, and a disabled man stood on the pavement holding a tray with matches and shoe laces for sale. These had probably disappeared by the end of 1947.

The Seven Sisters –
my mother is second
from the left.
From left to right
they are : Muriel,
Rose, Edith, Phyllis,
Doris, Cissie, and
Evelyn

134

CIDER MAKING

Hacknell was noted for cider making, having a pruned and productive orchard, cider press, cellar and plenty of willing helpers to drink the finished product. An old horn beaker was upturned on the barrel ready for the next drinker – it was reckoned that the alcohol sterilized it! I am not sure how many gallons were made in a good year; the talk was of hogsheads and barrels. A hogshead is approximately sixty gallons; the barrels were big, probably three to four hogsheads, and there were quite a few barrels or casks, depending on late spring frosts. Some years very little cider was made and in disastrous years, none!

Late autumn, after dessert apples had been picked and stored, was the time to be dealing with cider apples, distinct varieties grown for that purpose only, they were sour and dry. A proportion of windfall dessert and cooking apples could be added, but too many Bramleys made a very sour cider.

Those that had not fallen were knocked down with sticks, gathered up in baskets, and bagged ready to be loaded into carts or later a trailer, taken to outside the pound house at the entrance to the yard, where the apple crusher had been brought out for its annual airing. This crusher was a wooden box with sloping sides, two square rollers at the base were turned by a handle on the side, later by a belt connected to a pulley on the tractor, the whole stood on an iron frame.

Apples were tipped into the box, prodded down with a large wood mallet and crushed by the rollers, the resulting pomace sliding down a wood chute into trays below. The press had been prepared with a layer of oat straw extending well beyond the four sides of the square base, pomace was spread on this straw inside the base area, the over-hanging straw brought into the centre enfolding the pulp and ends tucked into it. More straw was laid on, repeating the process until the resulting "cheese" was high enough, or all the apples used. At this stage the square top was revolved downwards on the thick central iron shaft with deeply cut thread. Able to be turned by hand before settling on the cheese, more pressure had to be applied using a short pole, one end made to fit into an iron box, part of the mechanism turning on the shaft. Only enough pressure to make the liquid flow was needed, too much would burst the rolled straw. This squeezing continued for some hours, the short pole being replaced by a longer one for more leverage, for it took a great deal of strength to press the cheese to maximum tightness.

Abie and John Eastman
making the cheese

During this time, the liquid which strained through the straw ran down into the trough surrounding the base to flow out through a short chute into a wooden container called, I believe, a keeve, holding something like five gallons. The sweet or unfermented cider was dipped from the keeve and poured by the bucketful into a funnel inserted in the bung hole of a cask laid on its side. When the cheese had stopped running, the sides were trimmed down with a hay knife; the top pressure released enough to be able to throw the resulting trimmings on the top before squeezing down again; this was repeated several times until the cheese finished up as a very small block, guzzled with relish by the pigs.

Bernie and I loved this sweet cider straight from the press, not alcoholic at that stage, but strong enough to make a little girl sleep for hours under a cart in the cart linhay, and syrup of figs unnecessary! The fermenting cider produced a beard of white foam up through the bung hole and down the side of the cask, when the fermentation had stopped the cider was "racked" off into a clean barrel and allowed to stand until deemed fit to drink. There was never a shortage of volunteers to sample and pass judgment.

A few other farmers brought apples to Hacknell to make their own cider; one I especially remember is Bob Underhill from Higher Week, because he used to bring dandelions and "milky dashels" (thistles) for my rabbits.

At Week, the press was at ground level and the keeve sunk into a pit; using this with difficulty for one season, Dad returned to Hacknell for his remaining cider-making years.

John tipping apples into the crusher

137

Lark and Spot off for a drive

Jenny – one of our many tortoiseshell & white cats

HORSEPOWER, DOGS AND CATS

Horses

Having lived through the time of transference from horses to tractors as the source of energy on the vast majority of farms, and not having experienced the hard work they entailed, I remember them only with nostalgia.

I enjoyed many rides with Granfer taking flatpols, mangels, turnips or swedes to the sheep in spring with horse and butt; he sat on one front corner holding the reins, I on the other, holding tight. We had Tidy, a brown, cob sized mare, Charlie, a big long-legged brown and white horse, Snug and Prince, a pair of blacks with white blaize and Tommy, big, sturdy and brown was Tidy's colt – a young horse, and the one I remember the most because he came with us to Week. He was good natured but headstrong. When turned for home, he went straight through the rails by the lower gate of Sandpark at Hacknell and trotted up across Week Down, with me bouncing up and down on his back, just a bag to sit on, hauling on to the reins. Luckily the gate onto the road was shut.

Tommy with Dad

139

When Uncle Albert Way died, his pony, Queenie, came to Week and lived to a great age. She was reliable in a trap – his only means of transport – and would carry him all day hunting. She stayed out all the winter, growing a thick furry coat in the autumn which kept her warm. She was brought into the stable for one night during the severe 1963 winter and spent all night kicking the door to get out! When the hounds were within hearing she would get so excited, racing round and round the field, not at all like a thirty year old horse should behave.

Every morning the milk churns were loaded into the horse butt and taken to the stand at the top of the lane. At Hacknell, being such a long lane and both farms down it sending milk, the journey was shared, I think weekly, with Mr. Bill Mills. Sometimes the driver was his brother, John, who apart from constantly clicking out of the side of his mouth at the horse, never hurried it, so the horse soon got wise to this and took longer and longer each day; a leisurely journey for both.

One morning, the churns were heard rattling in the distance, the horse trotting into Hacknell yard, John Mills hardly able to hold it still while our churns were loaded, then off up the lane in record time, no need for John to click encouragement. Bill Mills had put some kind of oil on the horses hooves, used normally as medication, which warmed them so the horse kept moving to cool his feet.

The collection of milk in churns ceased in August, 1978 and a tractor replaced the horse long before then. Again at Week we shared transport with our neighbour, Bill Underhill; every other week he would pick ours up with his Allis Chalmers, an ungainly looking tractor with a high seat and long steering column – our David Brown looked small and neat beside it. The milk was collected at various times from 7.00 a.m. to mid-day, depending on how the round was arranged. This was no problem in the winter, but mid-day at harvest time certainly was; taken up early to stand in hot sun for hours resulted in churns of milk being returned as "of poor keeping quality". Delayed until the correct time, it was easily forgotten before the noise of metal churns clattering on a metal bottomed lorry at

Upcott or Deptford, panicked that day's delivery man into a mad rush of loading and dashing up the lane before the lorry left.

Through the years horses had died or been sold, as a natural happening, but the sale of Tommy was different. It was the end of an era, our last working horse. It was a sad day when he walked up the transport ramp going off to I, at least, knew not where.

Dogs

There have been many well-loved and lovely dogs down through the years. At Hacknell, Abie's spaniel, Chloe, helped me learn to walk. Pulling myself up by gripping her fur, I would lean on her while she walked slowly forward. At least once she nuzzled me over and picked me up by my clothes, taking me indoors away from the danger in the yard – so I have been told.

Jim Patt, an old English sheepdog, named after his previous owner, was shorn at sheep shearing time to relieve him of his thick matted coat during the hot days of summer. From looking butch and stocky before his coat came off, he looked slim and comical for a while after – but still strong enough to work the sheep.

Jock

Jock was a small border collie Dad bought from one of Gerald Champion's cattle transport drivers for £3.50 soon after we came to

Week. He was good with cattle as well as sheep but gentle enough to help Mum round up the turkeys, geese and ducks to shut them in, safe from foxes.

These faithful companions were laid to rest in the orchard as were bottle fed tame sheep, Lizzie, Mary and Jenny and remembered with affection.

Cats

Having loved cats all my life, I could not imagine a home without one or two favoured felines curled up on a cushion or before the fire. Generations of black and white cats called Topsy and black ones called Tony blend into each other but there were others who stood out from the crowd. Besides some already recorded, there was Kitty, a grey tabby who soon learnt to suck the lambs' bottle for an extra feed. Rasher who relished raw runner beans and another Bonzo, a large ginger tom, who could jump onto a wood-framed conservatory at Week and from there leap up to the bedroom window sills, almost causing heart attacks when the occupants spotted these wide open, shining eyes staring in.

In the early fifties we were given two kittens by the Snell family at Prospect, High Bickington. Patch a short-haired tortoiseshell and white, and a ginger female. Patch was the matriarch of a dynasty of tortoiseshell and white cats who were always such individual, independent characters. Daughters followed mothers for over forty years until cat leukemia and F.I.V. wiped out all the descendants in the mid-1990s. So, until we are sure that the disease has died out with the two remaining farm cats, there will be no contented purring heard in our kitchen.

PIG KILLING

Suffice to say, without going into the gory details of pig killing, that I hated those weeks, usually two or three times between September 1st and April 30th; only two a year in wartime. This sacrificial animal would have been either bought, if no home produced pig was available, or singled out from the fully grown litter of our sow, then the rest sold.

Pigs at Hacknell had the run of a sloping grassy plot below the farmyard, all the rain water and "flete" – the run off from the dung pit – ran down through this plot as well as the drainage from the house; this was a kind of natural cesspit! Needless to say the pigs loved it, muzzling up what little grass grew there and wallowing in the mud and muck.

The chosen one was removed from this squalor, shut in a house to be fattened up, fed liberally with barley meal, boiled potatoes and surplus milk, all mixed together into a sloppy feed, to which a special fattening meal bought from agricultural merchants was added. Washing up water, without soap, would be kept in a bucket for this purpose to supplement the milk. Overweight and pampered, some pigs would become very tame. One called Simon loved to have his back scratched and lie on his side to have his tummy rubbed. These pigs were reared to an enormous size, probably four times as big as regarded killing size now, bedded with plenty of straw to keep them clean and comfortable.

I hated the ear-piercing squealing when the pig was taken unwillingly from its house for my father to slaughter swiftly. I hated the smell of the carcass being scraped clean by pouring gallons of boiling water over it, an area at a time, until every bit of hair was removed. The legs were scalded one at a time by inserting them into the mouth of a two gallon earthenware pitcher half full of boiling water, pincers were used to pull off the nails to complete the cleaning operation. Now came the time to haul the carcass from the pig's form (a bench with four legs and four handles) using a "gammer" (a wooden brace between the back legs) to hang it up clear of the floor so it could be disemboweled into the large galvanized wash tray waiting below.

Carried quickly into the house, Mum and Gran began immediately to separate the small intestines from the caul – the fat veined veil that held them together – by cutting very carefully with scissors. With one person holding the looped intestines over a bucket, another cut the lowest point to empty them. I was press-ganged into helping Granny do this when I was older. Now came the start of washing these, roughly six foot, lengths; easy at Hacknell with a water tap indoors but a different matter at Week with water in buckets carried from the well! Repeatedly being washed and turned inside out with a smooth thumb-thickness stick before returning to fresh salt water over two days.

The pig was jointed or cut up the day after slaughter, the thick layer of fat cut from the pork; any bits of meat on the underside of the fat bacon were sliced off, these we called pork steaks, delicious fried the same day. Sometimes this bacon was four inches thick, crisp and dry when fried, beloved by Mr. W. E. Short, of Hill Crest, who lived to be a hundred.

Odds and ends of pork were cooked, minced, seasoned and added to cooked groats to fill the six foot skins with a spout screwed to the mincer, tied twice every six inches or so, the hogs puddings were lowered into a pan of boiling water to cook, then hung over a stick to dry and cut singly when fried. Any surplus intestines were cut into short lengths and fried, these were known as chitterlings or natlings. The lightly cooked liver was chopped with bacon, herbs and seasoning, wrapped in squares of caul to make faggots. Joints of pork and hogs pudding were exchanged with neighbours, providing a supply of fresh pork throughout the winter, for without freezers or fridges, salting or brine was the only method of preserving.

We used the dry salt method for the pork and bacon. Rubbed well all over with salt and layered in salt in large earthenware salters or wooden trenells in the dairy, these joints would be soaked for a day before cooking. The trotters, knuckles and head were cleaned and cooked before being made into brawn.

Two important factors decided the date to kill the pig. Apart from there being an R in the month, the moon was to be waxing (growing) otherwise the meat would shrink when cooked; (should we ask the butcher or supermarket if their pork fits this standard?). Another factor being that if, for any lady involved in the preserving, it was that, then unmentionable, "certain time of the month", she must not touch the bacon or pork, otherwise it would not keep, for the palm of the hand was thought to be warmer at that time.

This was not, as you might think, an easy opt out, for no doubt she was the one to render down the lard to be strained into "steans" – earthenware pots – and wash all the greasy dishes besides the cooking of faggots and hogs pudding.

For us children, the gift of the pig's bladder to be blown up and used as a football gave us much pleasure and removed us away from fidgety adults for a while.

Pig killing was a mammoth task for any household but especially so at Hacknell with eight people, rising to eleven with the evacuees, to be fed every day, whatever other jobs came along.

October Triplets

Our first David Brown Tractor, with double seat.
Bernie is driving, with father next to him.

WHEN WE CAME TO WEEK – AND TODAY, APRIL 2001

The Foundation Account at April 5th, 1946, shows my parents began with cattle worth £178 16s 0d, poultry £68 4s 6d and sheep £76 4s.9d – a total stock-in-trade of £323 5s.3d. With implements purchased from January to March worth £121 13s 6d, and a car valued at £15 0s 0d, their total assets were £459 18s 9d

Soon after that date, farm wages were £3 5s 7d after deductions for insurance etc., so my father's weekly earnings at Abbotsmarsh prior to that could not have been more than this amount – little opportunity to save a great deal, so borrowing was considerable.

By the March 1947 Balance Sheet, stock-in-trade was valued at £1,384 17s 6d, the increase gained by the addition of more stock, i.e "cow and calf from J. Laramy at £50 0s 0d;" "2 yearlings at £24;" "£6 1s 0d day-old chicks from Stirling;" "£3 15s 0d – ducks from Cecil Squire;" just some of the stock bought, and the original sheep and cattle, being one year older, were more valuable. More implements and tools had been bought, raising this value to £335 0s 0d. Having hired a tractor from the War Ag: (W.A.E.C.) for a certain number of days in early 1946, at a cost of £12, our first tractor, a Fordson Major, was purchased from Mr.Crocker in March '47 for £335.

No doubt some sheep came from Hacknell, given the continuing system of selecting the best ewe lambs for replacing older ewes for lambing the next year; they would have been descendants of those brought to Hacknell from Shuteley Farm, High Bickington. And so it has been down through the years. By the time Eric and I married in 1956, Dad was so badly affected by arthritis he needed two walking sticks to get around. So, this task of selecting thirty to forty ewe hogs (hoggetts) has been Eric's since that time, with Hazel's help after she left school until the roles were reversed as Eric became less agile.

When Hazel married David in 1996, Eric gladly left all the sheep handling to them. So although not a pedigree flock, the bloodlines went back many years not only in our own flock but in that of David and Kathleen's, for each year they bought replacement ewe hogs from us.

We saw no reason for this pattern to change, until April 10th 2001 when we became case number 121 of Foot and Mouth disease in Devon. Having been living on a knife-edge for seven weeks – as had every other farmer in Devon and other areas – the shock was still considerable. That day seemed endless, yet so much happened swiftly and entirely beyond our control.

On April 5th we had heard of Peter and Marilyn Smales' confirmed outbreak, with sorrow and compassion for them and for the people of Burrington having to endure the sight and smell of rotting carcasses for days on end.

Beyond our control, and a very sad part for us, was the inevitable involvement of adjoining neighbours – the Downs at Deptford, Kathleen and David, Colin Miller, Robert May, Liz and Brian Griffiths, the Elworthys at Upcott, Stan and Una Parker's land at Bales Ash, Dick and Margaret Beaumont at Week Park and Pat Andrews at Higher Week and others who were yet to be involved. All are our friends, some for a life-time, for Elworthys were at Upcott and Downs at Deptford before we came to Week.

By the end of that day – April 10th – we were all devastated, especially Hazel and David, having helped to slaughter sixty-six bullocks, four hundred and fifteen ewes, nine rams, plus more than six hundred lambs; lambs I had watched skipping around their mothers when I looked out of the window in the morning, knowing that would be the last time. Another sadness on April 10th was that Eric's cousins at Lordsdown, South Molton went down with Foot and Mouth on that day.

The Ministry vets and slaughter team did their jobs as well as they were able, with care and consideration.

April 11th dawned a beautiful morning, almost insensitively bright for the gruesome sight of piles of dead sheep lying in the fields and the yard full of dead bullocks, already blown up to bursting point, and the slaughter team coming again to kill all Kathleen and David's sheep in the afternoon. Fly, our sheepdog, was very subdued afterwards; she must have thought it strange to keep driving flocks into pens but not away again.

Mornings came and days went by without the need to think of animals being fed, or checked for lameness or looking poorly. We had a silence around us, a dog with no work, hay silage and straw with nothing to feed or bed, an already overpowering smell everywhere which we knew we had to live with for at least two weeks, because although we hoped the animals would be buried at Week Down, we were only given the choice of a funeral pyre or rendering.

Believing that the pyres were a source of spreading the disease, we did not wish to inflict that on further neighbours – and on our conscience, this was our only option.

Since the start of lambing in early January I had been waiting for the day when the kitchen windowsill would be free from bottles, teats, jugs and a box of milk powder to feed orphan lambs; when that day came, how I wished them back again.

We were very comforted by so many phone calls, letters, cards, offers to shop, collect things and cheering gifts. The box at the end of the lane became our lifeline while we continued as virtual prisoners here.

Sheep in winter

People we will remember long after the disease has been conquered are:-

☞ Nick Brown for his constant assurance that it was "under control," when to everybody else it obviously was not.

☞ Tony Blair for his empty promises and determination to play it down so that it did not upset his suspected election plans.

☞ Anthony Gibson, the N.F.U. South West Region spokesman, for his honestly considered reporting of the crisis daily on television and radio, his obvious distress for all farmers and their animals, and understandable frustration with inefficient M.A.F.F. and Government officials for bureaucracy and delaying tactics whilst the disease spread like wild fire.

Fly – 2001

AUGUST 2001

Four months after the nightmare of Foot and Mouth disease, still the stress continues with the restrictions of being a Form A premises and the fastidious requirements of the clean-up operation after animals were removed – our sheep in the fields on the sixteenth day and those in the yard, plus sixty-six bullocks on the eighteenth day after slaughter.

Like ripples in a pond, other neighbours became involved. Ruth and Alan Govier, Susan and Clifford Ley lost all their stock – Clifford having survived the worst known floods last winter – Roger and Angela Snell, Dick and Evelyn Martin had sheep slaughtered in outlying fields, adjoining infected farms, but were able to keep those nearer home, as had Stanley Parker.

For weeks our only visitors were white boiler-suited M.A.F.F. officials overseeing the rigorous programme of cleaning and disinfecting imposed on us. Checking the diary of daily work and collecting the weekly time sheets. Farmers filling in time sheets? Unbelievable for men and women used to working to the needs of animals and dictates of the weather, regardless of the hours taken.

Centuries of cobwebs under high roofs could not resist the blast of pressure washing. Timbers now look like new wood. Back walls of sheds have been seen again after fifty years; anything burnable was burnt, along with the remaining hay, straw, sheep cake and barley.

Earth floors in the lambing sheds were dug up and replaced by lorry loads of chalk from Dorset, spread, sprayed and rolled many times to achieve a smooth surface, the pole structure stripped of any bark.

The ancient household dump in the orchard, used by previous occupiers, and by us until refuse collecting became available, had to be cleared, the contents buried along with other rubbish.

Something akin to tales of sailors being detailed to scrub decks with a toothbrush – farmers have been told to use steel wool, emery and sand paper, pocket knives, etc. to reach a level of sterile cleanliness to satisfy inspecting vets – one or two stages above our regular cleaning officer – and now D.E.F.R.A. (Department for Environment, Food and Rural Affairs – replaced M.A.F.F.) is surprised at the cost of it all – calling a halt to cleaning while an enquiry is held.

Having been given permission to plough two fields, a few weeks after sowing we were told that we would not be allowed to harvest them! This order has now been rescinded – a whole book could be written of bureaucracy in overdrive.

Not only have the farmers who lost their stock suffered, those who were able to keep their animals, but lived in this extensive infected area of Devon, have had to contend with the most awful problems, greatly increased expenses and receiving very depressed prices at the end of it.

Fly, our sheepdog, chases birds in the air for fun and exercise. She even has an occasional game of football with Didi, a lurcher. She has had no opportunity to practise her shepherding skills since April, but we hope she will be eager to work when there are sheep once more at Week.

"When we came to Week" could have its ending being written now, but knowing the resilience of farmers and their families, I doubt this will be the end for the majority. We sincerely pray that our neighbours will be our neighbours for many more years. We thank them and numerous friends for their love and support, not just at the present time but over many years through times of joy and sorrow, and hope that in the not too distant future they will again be farmers and custodians of the countryside.